WELCOME TO THE REAL WORLD

A dangerous place to be caught unprepared!

By Bryan Scott Williams
Certified Instructor and Trainer

Copyright © 2005 by Bryan Scott Williams

ISBN 0-7414-2623-4

Published by

INFINITY
PUBLISHING.COM

1094 New DeHaven Street, Suite 100
West Conshohocken, PA 19428-2713
Info@buybooksontheweb.com
www.buybooksontheweb.com
Toll-free (877) BUY BOOK
Local Phone (610) 941-9999
Fax (610) 941-9959

∞

Printed in the United States of America

Printed on Recycled Paper

Published June 2005

About the Website

As the purchaser of this book,
you are encouraged to visit our website located at

www.wa-protective.com

The website contains additional information about the
services we offer, contact information and more.

ABOUT THE AUTHOR

Bryan Scott Williams has been actively involved in law enforcement, close security, and professional firearms training for over 18 years. In 1995, he received a commendation for bravery from the Lake Housatonic Authority Marine Police. He has spent more than 15 years providing instruction and consulting services to private, corporate, military and law enforcement personnel in the use of weapons and specialized tactics, including assisting thousands of applicants in obtaining their state pistol permits.

In November of 2000, Williams was accepted to the Connecticut State Police Firearms Advisory Council, where he maintains a seat in good standing and acts as a consultant on pending legislation and other issues related to the use of firearms.

As a certified NRA training counselor, Williams is authorized by the National Rifle Association to certify new NRA firearms instructors. He is also an authorized instructor through the New Hampshire Department of Public Safety, authorized to certify security personnel, and the State of Utah Department of Public Safety, authorized to certify applicants for their Utah Concealed Carry Pistol Permits.

Williams has trained with a variety of sources, including the National Rifle Association, the Heckler & Koch International Training Division, and DEF-TEC Corporation's Law Enforcement Training Division. In addition, he has trained with former and active members of some of the most elite counter-terrorist organizations in the world, including the British and New Zealand SAS and the U.S. Navy S.E.A.L.'s.

An accomplished NAUI Master Level Scuba Diver, Williams is also certified in underwater rescue techniques and is a certified Emergency Medical Technician, licensed by the State of Connecticut. He has served for 18 months as the chief training officer for a local volunteer ambulance corps with responsibility for both the design and implementation of training programs for other personnel.

Williams' membership affiliations include the National Tactical Officers Association, the National Rifle Association and the American Society of Law Enforcement Trainers.

CONTENTS

10 September 2001

It was just like any other day. We awoke, wiped the sleep from our eyes and prepared for the day ahead. We sent our children off to school and headed to work. Returning to our homes that evening, we wrapped up our day and prepared for the next one. But the next day was 11 September 2001. The next day would be different.

The first plane struck the North Tower of the World Trade Centers at 8:46 a.m. My phone rang. "Are you watching the news?" asked the voice on the other end. I quickly turned on the television and watched countless reruns of the first plane as it impacted the North Tower of the World Trade Center. I was sure it was an accident. Then at 9:02 a.m., the second plane struck the South Tower. I realized immediately that this was no accident. Our country was under attack.

At 9:38 a.m. a third plane plowed into the Pentagon. At 10:30 a.m., a fourth plummeted into a field in Pennsylvania.

As a professional instructor and consultant who deals with people who are concerned about violent crimes and their own personal safety every day, those scenes of destruction will be burned forever in my mind. 11 September 2001, destined to be known from that point forward simply as 9/11, marked the day the world changed.

It also marked the day when the average citizen of the United States came to understand that events of terrorism are not restricted to other parts of the world, and we are not invulnerable, and as a nation must be eternally vigilant. We must be prepared to fight, if necessary, and win; whether we are confronted by a foreign terrorist or a domestic threat. That's why I wrote this book.

INTRODUCTION

According to a U.S. Department of Justice report on violent crime, an estimated five out of six Americans will become victims of violent crime at least once in their lives. That same study indicates that 40% of all Americans will be injured in an assault or robbery. And that was the picture *before* 11 September 2001.

Since then, the world has become an even more dangerous place, particularly for Americans. To make matters worse, fear mongering has caused would-be self-defense "experts" to crawl out of the woodwork in order to take your money for providing nothing more than a crash course in creating a false sense of security.

The material in this book is intended to provide you with an alternative to expensive seminars and fly-by-night consultants. It is designed to provide you with the tools you need to increase your awareness of your surroundings, assess potential threats, and develop techniques for diffusing potentially violent situations with minimal personal risk.

Please understand, no one is suggesting that you live in a perpetual state of paranoia. However, a majority of people today are living at the polar extremes of readiness--they're either suspicious of everyone who doesn't look just like them or they are completely oblivious to their own immediate surroundings. As a result, when a real danger appears they are often so overwhelmed with fear and/or shock that they become virtually helpless. And it is this helplessness which makes them the perfect victim.

On the morning of 11 September 2001, the crew and passengers of American Airlines Flight 93 understood the danger of helplessness. A handful of passengers chose to defend themselves rather than meekly accept the will of terrorists. In a perfect world, they would have found a way to overpower the terrorists and land the aircraft safely. Instead, their plane crashed into the Pennsylvania countryside. But just think what would have happened if the terrorists had been completely successful in their efforts? U.S. Intelligence sources say the terrorists intended to plunge that plane into the White House. The Arabic television station, Al-Jazeera, claims the target was the U.S. Capitol building. Either way, innumerable lives were saved because the passengers of American Airlines Flight 93 chose to take action.

The purpose of this book is to give you the knowledge and confidence you need to assess threats and deal with them-- not just terrorist threats--but the day-to-day threats many of us face but are rarely prepared for: street thugs, psychotic employees, enraged former spouses, home invaders, stalkers, rapists, drug-crazed thieves, carjackers and the like.

While no one can guarantee that this book will enable you to diffuse every possible threat to your safety, I can guarantee that you will be better prepared to do so if you apply the principles and techniques outlined herein.

HOW IT FEELS TO TAKE A BULLET

"That which does not kill us makes us stronger."

The story I am about to relate is from my own personal experience. On 21 February 1987, just before 8:00 p.m., I experienced the effects of a projectile entering my body and passing through it. In other words, I was shot. I won't go into the events that led to this incident, as I do not feel they are germane, and we'll discuss prevention techniques later. But it is important to understand what you are trying to avoid; that is, why you're studying this material in the first place. It's all too easy to minimize the impact of such an event; especially when TV and movies so often portray shootings so casually. So for the sake of getting real, so to speak, I'd like to give you a first-hand glimpse into what taking a bullet really means.

It is said that when a bullet enters the body it may not be noticed immediately. Hard to believe, but it's true. Fortunately, the injury I sustained did not strike a bone or any major organs or blood vessels. Instead, it struck a series of nerves, which to this day causes an atrophic feeling much like pins and needles in the region where the wound occurred.

The first feeling I experienced was a slight numbness in the region. I was aware that a shot had been fired, because I heard it. But it was not immediately apparent that I had been hit. I then started to sweat, but only in one area of my body. Due to the effects of shock, which is an automatic response resulting from severe bodily trauma; it took a minute for me to realize what had happened. I remember trying to piece it all together: I heard a shot, I felt some localized numbness, I was sweating but only in one area of my body. When it finally occurred to me to check myself, I put my hand over the area where the numbness had set in and realized it was covered in blood. Immediately, I tore open my clothing and observed a hole, approximately 1" in diameter.

My prior training told me that the dark color of the blood meant I was losing venous rather than arterial blood, which was definitely a good thing. Arterial blood is lighter in color, would have been pumping out much faster and would have been considerably more life threatening. Again, because I had been trained to think even in the most difficult circumstances, I knew enough to apply direct pressure to the area, which I immediately did. Then I entered my car and drove at a very high rate of speed to the nearest hospital. In hindsight, this was probably not the best idea I have ever had, but I was in shock so I'll chalk it up to that.

The next scene is somewhat reminiscent of a bad movie or a *Saturday Night Live* skit. I entered the hospital Emergency Room, white as a ghost, I'm sure, and trailing blood. A triage nurse saw me and asked as nonchalantly as you like "Can I help you?" My response was "I have been shot, you stupid bitch." Which normally I would not have done, except under the circumstances and the casual consideration I was being afforded I felt justified in my comments. The nurse then placed me in a wheelchair and wheeled me into the examination room.

Next the surgeon arrived. With no pain medication or even an offer of any, I was subsequently cajoled, poked and prodded. To check the track of the wound, the surgeon inserted his fat finger into the hole from which the bullet had escaped. The pain was indescribable. In spite of my screams for either pain medication or a break, the surgeon continued to poke around until he was satisfied that he'd gotten whatever information he could from torturing me, then told me he needed to irrigate the wound. Again, I requested pain meds. Again I was ignored.

He then pushed a large eyedropper filled with peroxide into the wound and squeezed until all the liquid had entered my body. The burning sensation it created was indescribable.

When the eye-dropper had been emptied and the bulb at the end was released, the liquid, blood and chunks of flesh returned to the shaft of the instrument, leaving me feeling as if I had just experienced the absolute maximum amount of pain it is possible to feel without simply passing out. After all of this, I was finally medicated and allowed to rest.

Over the next four days my wound was continually monitored and the dressing regularly changed. On the fifth day I was well enough to be sent home. I was given instructions to wash out the wound channel three times each day using a normal saline solution. After each cleansing, I changed the wound dressing. This was supposed to prevent infection. It didn't. Three days after I arrived home I developed a very nasty rash. The entire area around the wound, in a circumference of 8 to 9 inches, was bright red, seriously inflamed and was incredibly itchy.

After a visit to the surgeons office, I was ordered to return to the hospital, immediately, where I was told that I had developed something called *cellulitis*, a serious bacterial infection of the skin; which can, if untreated, become life threatening. Cellulitis begins as a red area that feels hot and tender. It also tends to spread rapidly. And while the infection may be superficial, it may also affect the tissue under the skin and can even spread to the lymph nodes and get into the bloodstream. Left untreated, the spreading bacterial infection may rapidly become a life-threatening condition. As a result, I was put on high volumes of intravenous antibiotics, and due to the large dosage required, the medication burned going in, making me feel as if my veins were on fire.

But even that didn't stop the infection. So the next step was to implant a drain. This was yet another adventure in testing my tolerance for pain as it involved an incision being made between the entry and exit wounds and the insertion of tubes in both wound sites. Due to the depth of the incision and my increasing tolerance for pain medication, the local anesthetic meant to make the procedure bearable didn't work as well as planned. I could actually feel the initial incision and the tubes as they were inserted into the wounds and the pulling and cutting of the tubes as they were positioned. Then I endured three more days of continued irrigation with saline. Still, the infection persisted.

It was finally decided that pieces of torn flesh within the wound channel were the cause of the infection and in order to heal, the wound would need to be surgically opened and allowed to "granulate." This meant the wound channel would be left open and the tissue would be allow to air out and heal from the inside out.

This also meant that I was to endure yet another cleaning process. Suffice it to say that when an instrument that can only be described as a cheese grater is inserted into the wound channel and used to scrape excess flesh from the wound area, it is painful beyond words. When I finally lost control and began attempting to fight the doctor off, I was sedated.

Now I will admit that my relationship with the surgeon in question was not a good one. In fact, when I was first admitted to the hospital I made the mistake of asking for anyone but him--and I paid dearly for that mistake. But the point is simply this: no matter who you are, no matter who is running the E.R., you do not want to get shot.

And this brings me to the final point of this story: it's not enough to survive a violent conflict--you must win at all cost. If anybody is going to take a bullet, let it be your attacker and not you.

SITUATIONAL AWARENESS

"Situational awareness is defined as the ability to observe, process and compose reactionary countermeasures to a given potential situation or incident based upon pre-incident behaviors and signs."

There are hundreds of books on the market today covering self-defense tactics, techniques, and strategies. However, virtually all of these books focus on the actual conflict and provide, at best, only a minimal overview of the mechanics of situational awareness and personal threat assessment. Therefore we will discuss these all-important, yet often under-discussed topic areas now.

One of the most frightening experiences human beings can be exposed to is the threat of physical violence against themselves or a family member. The purpose of this section is to help you develop your personal sense of awareness in an effort to prevent a violent situation from occurring in the first place. By raising your daily awareness of your environment and increasing your ability to better read, understand and react to a potential confrontation, you will be able to perform your own personal threat assessments. This information is particularly important when faced with a decision involving the use of deadly force. Throughout this section, we will examine the major elements needed to effectively and properly gauge a potential threat, as well as the proper response to it. Please keep in mind that this material is not intended to be an all-inclusive catalogue of every possible event that might lead to a violent confrontation. Rather it is designed to provide you with a baseline of information and knowledge from which to build your personal reaction and response structure.

The first step in avoiding a violent confrontation is to be consciously aware of your surroundings at all times, what we call *situational awareness*. However, extreme caution must be exercised not to succumb to the effects of paranoia or perhaps an even more dangerous condition commonly referred to as "burnout" or "apathy." This can include a variety of symptoms such as increased fatigue, stress, denial, lack of interest, inability to concentrate, increased irritability, or simply an overall feeling of being down trodden. This condition occurs when one attempts to maintain an ultra-high level of alertness on a continuing basis without ever experiencing the release of an actual incident upon which to act. So while the need to raise our level of awareness is paramount to the principle of self-protection, striking an appropriate balance between excessive awareness and total lack of awareness is often difficult.

Here's a simple way to understand what is meant by an appropriate level of awareness. In this day of high-speed daily activities, between work, family, friends, etc., distractions abound. When you exit your vehicle to enter a store, office or perhaps even your home, where is your focus? If you're like most people, you are more interested in where you are going and what you are about to do than in what is occurring around you. Now this does not make you a bad person, but it does make you a potential victim, for it is during just these times that you are most likely to be attacked or confronted by a hostile individual. Remember, the individual who is intent on victimizing you has only two things on his mind: what he plans to do to you, and some possible apprehension about being caught. He has also likely scoped out the area ahead of time and he knows potential exit routes, what, if anything, you might pick up and use as a weapon in self-defense, etc. You, on the other hand . . .

Well, to make the point, let's try an exercise.

☐ Put a pen and paper in your purse, briefcase or pocket so you have it handy next time you drive somewhere.

☐ When you get to your next destination, go about your normal routine with your usual amount of thought.

☐ After you are out of your car and have walked to the next safest point, i.e., to your front door, office elevator, etc., stop a moment and write down everything you saw from the time you got out of your car until you reached the point where you are now.

☐ Now walk back outside and see how much you missed!

If you are average, you failed to identify over 80% of the items you walked right by just moments before. Why? Because most people tend to focus on their intentions rather than their current actions. This is a great exercise for training yourself to be more aware. Each time you perform this exercise you will increase your situational awareness. Before you know it, you will automatically be primed to notice your surroundings in much greater detail, and that's the first step to performing your own personal threat assessment.

Of course, situational awareness by itself it not enough. It is also important to know how to read the actions of others so that you can gauge the level of threat that might develop.

PERSONAL THREAT ASSESSMENT

"But he always seemed like such a nice man."

> *--What everybody said about*
> *serial killer John Wayne Gacey*

Now that we have discussed why and how to be situationally aware, we can move on to techniques for identifying real, perceived or potential threats. When most people hear the term *threat assessment* they often think of the function of a security specialist; and while it is true that the performance of a threat assessment is one of the responsibilities of a security specialist there is no reason why the average person cannot use the same principles in his own self-protection plan.

In this section we will explain how you can perform your own personal threat assessments. Let's begin with a couple of real-life scenarios.

- [ ] *Scenario 1*: You are walking alone on a deserted street at dusk. You are approached by a dirty, disheveled looking man who asks you the time. How do you feel? Are you concerned, maybe a little nervous? Frightened perhaps?

- [ ] *Scenario 2*: You are walking alone on a deserted street at dusk. You are approached by a handsome, sophisticated looking man in an expensive suit. He asks you the time. How do you feel? Are you comfortable? Inclined to be friendly? Relaxed?

If you're like most people, our first scenario made you a little nervous; whereas, the second scenario caused little or no anxiety. But what if I were to tell you that the individual in scenario 1 was actually a harmless person who was just down on his luck and posed absolutely no threat to you? What's more, what if I told you the man in scenario 2 was in fact a well-known criminal who is suspected of a series of brutal murders? How do you feel now?

The point of this exercise is not to question your perception of others; rather, it is to remind you that regardless of your perceptions, if a person is unknown to you, that person should be treated with caution until determined otherwise.

Here's another real-life story to elaborate this point. Many years ago I visited a client at his home. I was dressed casually, as is my habit: jeans, t-shirt, etc. My client had a habit also: he liked to pay in cash. So after we concluded our business I stuffed a wad of bills into my pocket and headed for a nearby jewelry store in search of a new Rolex. I was in a pretty posh neighborhood. When I entered the jewelry store I sauntered up to the counter to check out the various watches and noticed the clerks were all congregating in the back of the store, chatting. Nobody asked if I needed any help. After several minutes of browsing, I finally spoke up and asked one of the clerks to show me a particular watch. It was clear from her demeanor that she thought I was being a bit of a nuisance. Apparently, she assumed I was simply there to look, not to buy. Even after asking for her assistance, she seemed less than interested in helping me, but she did as I asked and pulled the watch I wanted to look at out of its case. But before she handed it to me, she walked to the other end of the store, getting as far as possible from the door. At that point, she signaled me to join her. Evidently, my request had converted me from a *bother* to a *thief* in her eyes. Obviously, there are procedures that should be followed when showing a very valuable item to a client. But I couldn't help but wonder, would she have used that procedure if I had been wearing a three-piece suit? Likely not.

The point is that we all tend to judge a book by its cover. But when it comes to your safety, never forget that there are people who appear to be safe, but have nothing but ill intent on their minds. Likewise, one may look like the very dregs of society and be one of the best people society has to offer.

Types of threatening behavior

Before we discuss the methods of assessing a potential threat, we should first understand the main types of threatening behavior. These behaviors include:

☐ *The Obvious Threat*—The obvious threat, as the name implies, represents any action or behavior that threatens. This includes the presentation of weapons. An example of an obvious threat would be a group of individuals who are shouting insults as they wave switchblades. Their behavior clearly indicates a desire to arouse fear or uneasiness.

☐ *The Implied Threat*—The implied threat is a bit more subtle. Let's say you are walking down the street and you see an average looking man heading your way. No immediate aggression is apparent, but as you get closer he begins to mimic your movements and block your path. While he has not said or done anything violent, clearly there is an implied threat. Another example of an implied threat would be the same scenario but rather than mimicking your movements and block your way he might approach you with flared nostrils, heavy and rapid breathing or some other sign of agitation.

☐ *The Potential Threat*—The potential threat can be tricky because you will not always have a clear sign that a threat exists; rather, you will base your assessment on a feeling or instinct that tells you there is a potential danger. While this sounds vague and unsettling, the more you practice your situational awareness exercise as described in the previous chapter, the more your instincts will work to serve you. Trust them. The worst thing that can happen is that you err on the side of caution. And that's a good thing. After all, there is a reason for the expression "Better safe than sorry."

Personal threat assessment tips

The first step in a personal threat assessment is understanding the behaviors and potential methodologies of your attacker. While all attackers are not the same, there are some patterns or signs you should be aware of. These are all things you can assess using your five senses, so the goal is to make your assessment while there is still enough distance between you and the aggressor to enable an escape, if necessary. Remember, distance is your friend.

The eyes

According to an ancient English proverb, the eyes are the windows to the soul. There are six basic eye signals that you can watch for to help you decide if the person walking toward you is likely to be a friend or a foe. Keep in mind that these are general signals and are not meant to be definite proof of a potential threat.

1. *Refusal to make eye contact*—this may be due to a possible feeling of guilt on the part of the would-be aggressor. Or perhaps he/she is simply feeling hesitant about what he/she is planning to do. Either way, this *could* be a sign that this particular individual means you harm.

2. *Rapid blinking*—rapid blinking is generally considered a sign of lying or nervousness. The average blink rate is about 20/minute. While some people naturally do blink at a faster rate, this is one more potential clue to a person's mental state. So keep that in mind.

3. *Excessive and/or rapid widening of the eyes*—this is also sometimes referred to as the "wild-eyed look," and it is generally accepted as an indication of fear or surprise. This behavior is often observed in extremely aggressive individuals and is associated with an increased likelihood of verbal or physical abuse.

4. *Scanning with the eyes*—scanning from side to side frequently indicates nervousness and can be a prelude to an attack. It may, in fact, represent the aggressor's own personal threat assessment in action: he's checking to see who else is nearby and might either try to rescue you, or act as a witness to his crime, should he follow through on his intent.

5. *The hard, fixed gaze*—this is also associated with aggression and is typically aimed at the potential objective or target of the intended violence.

6. *Glassy or glazed eyes*—when an individual has a glassy-eyed look it usually suggests that he/she is under the influence of some form of narcotic. And as drug addicts sometime resort to violent means to get the money necessary to keep up their habits, this sign should not be ignored.

The following scenario will help to demonstrate how what we've just covered can apply to a real-life situation. Let's say that while out walking one evening you are approached by a disheveled-looking man who asks for spare change. He is not behaving in any overtly aggressive or threatening manner but you notice that his eyes are glassy. You immediately assume that he's under the influence of drugs or alcohol. You politely refuse his request and turn to walk past him. You hear him mutter under his breath and when you turn back to see if he's speaking to you, you notice that his eyes are now much wider and he is scanning from side to side rapidly and is blinking more frequently than he was when you first encountered him. Again, you turn your back to him to walk away. Bad move. Never turn your back on a potential threat. You are too close to him to be out of danger. When your turn your back, he lunges at you, pulls you around and stabs you in the abdomen before stealing your wallet and running off. You spend the next month in the hospital, have a series of painful and complicated surgeries and are now the proud owner of the latest fashion craze . . . a colostomy bag.

Congratulations!

The lesson of this story is simple: always keep your eyes on a potential threat. Until you are far enough away to be out of reach, do not turn your back.

The voice

People often interpret yelling or screaming as a sign of aggression and assume that violence will follow. However, this is not always the case. Certainly, if someone is yelling threats or displaying other aggressive behaviors, violence is a possibility and should not be dismissed. But sometimes the venting of anger and release of energy that screaming provides actually *lessens* the potential for violence.

Let's take two dogs, for example. Say the first dog is barking loudly while wagging its tail and is looking in your direction but not specifically at you. The second dog, however, is totally silent but his gaze is fixed dead on you. Its tail is still and it is not displaying any over signs of aggression. Which dog do you think poses a greater threat? While both animals may be dangerous, if I were you I'd be more concerned about the second dog. Why? Because the first dog isn't really concerned with you. If he were, his gaze would be solidly fixed on you, not just aimed in your general direction. In other words, if he were concerned about you, he'd be looking at you like the second dog is. Human beings are similar in this way. The axiom "always be mindful of the small quiet ones" applies here. While it is not always the case, sometimes when a situation is escalating to violence, the one who demonstrates the least activity or outward frustration is the one who poses the greatest threat.

Here's an example. You accidentally bump into somebody on the street. You apologize, but that's not good enough for them. They become angry and begin to level insults at you. You shout back, never expecting the confrontation to escalate beyond a verbal interchange. Suddenly, the person you've been arguing with becomes totally silent. He shuts down completely. But he maintains his gaze directly at you. What should you expect next? A physical attack? Possibly. Why? Because the shut down phase represents the transition between expressing the anger and frustration of the moment and the decision to act on it.

The body

While the behaviors outlined above are clues to an individual's mental state, there are many more subtle forms of body language which can also tell us about the individual we are dealing with. There are seven basic body signals that you should be aware of.

1. *Violation of personal space*—Have you ever noticed that some people feel compelled to get right up in your face to talk to you? It can be a bit annoying, yet usually we don't feel overly threatened by it. Psychologists say that an average person requires a minimum of three feet of "personal space" around them to feel comfortable. And while we all know some people who like to get a little closer, as a rule, a violation of personal space by a person *unknown* to you is a sign of potential danger. The big question, of course, is when should you act on it? There is no set answer to that, I'm afraid, except to say that the best time to act is when you feel you are in grave danger of bodily harm and have the most confidence in your ability to do so successfully. It is also important to act in a way that will not further escalate the situation. For example, if a person violates your personal space but is not otherwise acting in an aggressive or threatening manner, the best response would be to simply take a step back in a casual, natural way. If, however, your instincts tell you that this person is a threat, then you must be prepared to respond with aggression. Unfortunately, no one can tell you when that is necessary, as that decision will be based on your own perception of danger based on your personal threat assessment. We'll get into that scenario in the chapter titled *Fight or Flight*.

2. *Hands on Hips*—This posture is usually associated with confidence or readiness but it can also be a sign of aggression. However, sometimes it is difficult to determine which is the case. For this reason it should never be used as a sole indicator of anticipated aggression; rather it should be used, like all the other tools in this chapter, as a piece of your overall assessment.

3. *Arms crossed over chest*—The action of crossing the arms across one's chest can have multiple meanings as well. For instance, when it's cold, it is not uncommon to see people cross their arms over their chests in an effort to warm themselves. In the context of a threat assessment, however, crossed arms may be expressing confidence as well as the potential for aggression.

4. *Hands clasped behind the back*—This stance is generally considered a bad move from a tactical perspective. However, it can also be a sign of anger, frustration or fear and should be taken into account during a threat assessment. While it may indicate nothing more than arrogance of an excess of confidence, there always exists the possibility that the hidden hands are actually hiding something--a weapon, perhaps. It could also indicate that the potential attacker is exceptionally skilled in martial arts and can use his legs and feet to attack, as well as his hands. Another possibility is that the he is attempting to lure you into a false sense of security, giving you the impression that he is relaxed and harmless. If this position is assumed in the middle of a heated argument, it is recommended that you immediately prepare for an attack or retreat from the area.

5. *Tapping or drumming fingers*—Another sign of aggression is the rapid or continuous drumming of the fingers. This is often associated with impatience or frustration and will usually not be a significant indicator of trouble by itself. However, as with the all of the behaviors listed here, if combined with other symptoms

of aggression, it may indicate a potential confrontation.

6. *The handshake*—The custom of shaking hands dates back to the time of the Roman Empire. When centurions would meet, they would shake hands to prove that they were not carrying weapons and to assure the other that they harbored no ill intent. Today, however, we must remember that in order to shake hands we need to be extremely close to the other individual. Therefore, the decision of whether or not to shake hands must be based upon your assessment of the other signs of aggression listed above. In short, a handshake offered by an unknown person, who is exhibiting signs of instability or aggression, should not be accepted unless you are quite sure you are dealing with a person who does not present a threat to you, or you are fully prepared to counter any attack which may occur.

7. *Brisk and erect gate*—When a person walks toward you with a brisk and erect gate he is demonstrating a form of aggression. While he may not be dangerous, this is clue to the mindset of the person who is approaching and should be part of your overall threat assessment.

While there are many body language clues that can be used to determine the intent of a person unknown to you, the list above contains those that, I believe, are most important for performing a *personal threat assessment*.

Putting it all together

As the title of this section suggests, the key to a successful personal threat assessment is the ability to put all these exercises, visual cues and threat assessment techniques together.

Practicing awareness of your surroundings and familiarizing yourself with visual indicators, such as a person's eye movements and/or body language cues, are all very important. But to get a real feel for how this fits together, let me share with you another real-life story of a violent confrontation unfolding. Take particular note of the visual cues and body language descriptions that helped me understand what I was dealing with as the situation evolved.

At the time of the incident, I was working at a nightclub in a dangerous part of town. As part of a security team, I was responsible for ensuring that no weapons or drugs made it into the club and for providing close protection to the owners of the club. In addition, I was expected to manage any confrontations that developed on the premises. On this particular night, the club was very busy but there were no conflicts or other problems. It was a warm night, so my partner and I decided to stand outside for awhile. While we were talking, we saw a young woman running up the opposite side of the street. She was screaming, "Help, he is going to kill me." Now, because we were not acting in the capacity of police, but were employees of a private club, we could not legally leave the grounds for the purpose of interfering, unless we observed an actual physical attack. At this point, all we saw was a screaming woman; therefore, we were legally obligated to stay where we were and simply observe.

The woman, who had noticed us watching her, saw that we were in uniform. She ran over to us and explained that her boyfriend was high on "ice" (*Crystal Methamphetamine*), an extremely powerful hallucinogenic narcotic compound which generally inspires acts of violence or aggression. She told us that they had been fighting and that he was going to kill her. We decided to call the police and offered to let her wait in the nightclub alcove until they arrived. This area was approximately 7' long and 6' wide and housed a cigarette machine which was positioned against the wall opposite the nightclub door. Due to the excessively loud music, coming from the club, my partner decided to go out to his van and use his car phone to contact the police, leaving me alone with the woman. Less than a minute after my partner left, the woman's boyfriend was observed walking up the other side of the street. He was obviously looking for her. I told her to stay put and assured her that he would not be able to find her. I also reminded her that the police would soon be on site. However, the woman decided to use me as a shield, and pushing past me, she yelled something unintelligible at her boyfriend, who turned toward us. She immediately turned and ran back into the alcove, with the boyfriend coming after her. To prevent them from entering the club, I placed my back to the club entrance door. When the boyfriend entered the alcove I asked him, politely, not to the escalate the situation further and to leave the premises. His response was "Fuck off." (Language intensity is a clue to potential violence, as stated earlier, so please do not be offended by my use of it here--it is meant to make a point).

I decided, based on a variety of indicators (including vocal cues, body language and my own instincts) that the best thing for me to do was to wait until the situation escalated to violence before attempting to use force. I didn't need to wait long. The boyfriend proceeded to grab the woman and slam her against the wall saying, "I am going to fucking kill you, you bitch." At this point I grabbed the boyfriend and told him to back off, pushing him away from the woman and toward the cigarette machine. He responded by calling me a series of colorful names, adding that he had a gun and was going to blow my head off. Immediately, I began to scan his body while, instinctively, my master hand went for my weapon and drew it from its holster. It was obvious from his eyes that he was under the influence of some form of drug and during his rant, as he began to flail his arms, I observed a pistol tucked into the front of his waistband. I realized that the situation was rapidly escalating to a level which, while prepared for, I did not wish it to go. So I took the opportunity to act aggressively while he was flailing about and struck him in the center of his chest while using my support hand to force him back against the cigarette machine. I raised my weapon, a Glock 17 (9mm semi-automatic pistol) and explained to him that while I did not wish to shoot him, I would do so, without hesitation, if he moved a muscle. He immediately ceased his moments and positioned his hands over his head, as all color left his face. My partner returned and assisted me with restraining this individual, which including removing a 2" 38 caliber revolver he'd been carrying. When the police arrived, they arrested him. He was subsequently charged, tried and convicted on a variety of charges.

However the story does not end there. Before the police (with whom my partner and I had a solid working relationship) arrived, we decided for our own safety, that we should handcuff the individual. Upon arrival of the police, a young officer prepared to take him into custody. I expressed to the officer that the individual was extremely violent and appeared to be under the influence of some narcotic. I also let him know that I felt it would be unwise to remove the handcuffs (which belonged to me), saying that I would pick them up later, at the police station. Unfortunately, I was ignored and this young officer released one side of my handcuffs without first applying his own. This caused a series of events which will not soon be forgotten. To begin with, the suspect now had a weapon. A weapon you ask? Yes, a weapon. One handcuff attached to the wrist of a violent individual is tantamount to giving him a knife; and by flailing his arms he presented a serious risk of injury to everyone within the immediate area.

Next, the officer lost his grip on the suspect, giving him the opportunity to run away, but it was immediately apparent that the suspect had other ideas. The suspect climbed up on the roof of the patrol car and began to jump up and down, breaking the light bar and caving in the roof. The ensuing commotion motivated several others to get involved and as a result, a miniature riot broke out. Bottles were thrown; gunshots were fired; basically, all hell broke loose. After all of this commotion was brought under control, the Lieutenant from the department approached me and asked what had happened.

When I told him, he simply walked away in disgust. The moral of this story is simply this: act as quickly as possible and do your best to control every encounter, or as I am known for saying, "Get in, do what you need to, and get the hell out". And don't forget: *distance is your friend and time is your enemy.*

Daily situational awareness tips

We've discussed threat assessment, cues you can use to understand the potential for a threat and the importance of moving quickly and with confidence when a threat is perceived. Now we're going to look at some very basic tips for maintaining situational awareness.

The following list offers some basic techniques which can, and should, be incorporated into your daily life to aid in your situational awareness. It's a very good idea to practice these every day. After all, you may not know ahead of time when you're going to need them.

☐ *Keep your distance when stopped in traffic.* Whenever you are stopped in traffic, keep a minimum of one car's length of distance between your vehicle and the vehicle in front of you. The reason for this is that in the event of a dangerous development (like a carjacker trying to get into your car) you can easily maneuver your vehicle and drive away. Don't let yourself be intimidated by the driver behind you, who may honk and motion for you to pull up. Your safety is much more important that the opinion of a rude stranger.

☐ *Take note of your surroundings.* We covered this under the *Personal Threat Assessment* section, but you really can't think about this too much. Regardless of whether you think you are in a dangerous environment, always pay attention to your surroundings. If something appears out of the ordinary, increase your defensive posture and stay alert. Think about how you might evacuate the area quickly if you should find yourself in danger. Practice this every day.

☐ *Keep your master hand free.* If you are left-handed, your master hand is your left hand. It's the one you can most easily control. So put your car keys in your right hand when you are walking toward your vehicle. This will keep your master hand free for action.

☐ *Use carts or other methods to avoid carrying packages that will obscure your vision or leave you without the ability to move quickly.* In a violent confrontation, seconds count. If you're burdened with packages, the time it takes to set them down and get your bearings might be time you don't have. What's more, if you have a cart with you, you may be able to conceal yourself behind it.

☐ *Avoid hugging walls.* When you're out on the sidewalk, avoid hugging the walls and stay closer to the curb. Hugging the wall can cause two problems: first, it restricts your ability for movement; second, it is easier for an attacker to conceal himself in alleyways, alcoves and entrances. If you hug the wall you will position yourself closer to potential areas of concealment.

While the preceding list is by no means all inclusive, it is intended to provide you with some guidelines which, if implemented on a regular basis, may help prevent a confrontation.

TERRORISM: A NEW TYPE OF THREAT

"A threat can only be countered by someone who understands the nature of the threat."

Prior to 11 September 2001, the average citizen of the United States had very little reason to be concerned with international terrorism. With few exceptions, foreign terrorists, even those determined to attack the United States, did so by targeting U.S. facilities abroad. Americans now understand that even on American soil, terrorism is a real possibility.

In this section, we will discuss the various types of terrorism and their implications.

Acts of foreign terrorism

While a handful of mass-casualty attacks did occur in the United States prior to 9/11, such as the incident at Columbine High School, they were generally isolated in nature and not part of a larger plan of action by an organized group of fanatics. In the wake of 9/11, however, we are now faced with an even more aggressive, violent, and insidious threat. That threat is posed by organized terrorist groups such as al-Qaeda, Hamas, Hezbollah, Islamic Jihad, and a host of other terrorist groups who, due to their radical political and/or religious points of view, have waged war on Americans, both at home and abroad.

When most people think of acts of terrorism, they think of political kidnappings, assassinations, car bombs, or other types of attacks that typically occur in other parts of the world. But what we know now is that the intention of these groups, as they have stated very clearly, is to attack Americans on American soil. They are waging what is known as a "Jihad" or "Holy War" against what they refer to as the "Infidels" or "Devils of the West," which places us all within their crosshairs.

I believe that protection against this type of threat requires a combined effort on the part of both the citizens and the government. Granted, there are threats which the average person will have no means of detecting or combating, such as any form of attack which comes from the use of a weapon of mass destruction. However, there are other forms of attacks which the average citizen can and should be aware of and be prepared to defend themselves against.

The following types of attacks were taken directly from an al-Qaeda training manual, and as such show the potential threats we face on a daily basis. However, with the proper situational awareness, combat mindset, and training, the chances of surviving such an attack will be increased significantly.

Mass shootings—This type of attack generally involves an individual or group opening fire on a large gathering of people at a fixed location, i.e. a school, corporate headquarters, a shopping mall, train/bus station, convention hall, or other highly populated areas. The purpose of a mass shooting is generally to kill as many as people as possible before being killed or otherwise subdued. Perhaps the most widely remembered case of this type of attack occurred in Columbine, CO, when a lone high school student opened fire in a student cafeteria. However, there have been many more cases of this type of attack.

Though not generally identified as such within the news media, a mass shooting is actually considered an act of domestic terrorism. In fact, to date there have been no cases of mass shootings on U.S. soil which have involved a foreign terrorist element. Yet the impact of this type of violence is much the same as with any terrorist attack. A *knee-jerk* reaction is the norm. This typically involves a general hysteria followed by the passage of irrational laws which impact only law abiding citizens and have virtually no impact on the terrorists.

These types of attacks are in many ways identical to the type of attacks observed around the world by our military, including ambushes against U.S troops in Iraq, attacks on Iraqi police forces and political kidnapping attempts. The difference is that, unlike a school shooting or other single issue attack, these attacks will generally be part of a larger planned action, and in some cases will be used as a diversionary tactic to defer attention, or otherwise occupy personnel, to prevent them from responding to another simultaneous event.

Suicide bombing—Since the invasion of Iraq, attacks by so called "suicide" or "homicide" bombers in the United States have been of particular concern. Prior to the Iraq war, attacks of this kind were only common in the Middle East, particularly in Israel. However, in May of 2004, during the lead-up to the presidential election, the FBI sent out a bulletin to 18,000 law enforcement agencies around the country warning of an increased possibility of suicide bombings within the U.S. The concern stemmed largely from the fear that al-Qaeda would attempt to launch an attack here in the U.S. in an effort to influence the presidential elections, just as they did in Spain with the Madrid train bombings; which were followed by the defeat of President Aznar and the withdrawal of Spanish troops from Iraq. This type of attack is considered a *low level* attack; whereas, the attacks on 9/11 are considered *high level* attacks. As you may have guessed, the level of an attack is based on several criteria, the main three are: number of dead, the amount of physical damage done, and the type of weapon used.

Another relatively new tactic that Islamic terrorists are using more and more is that of employing women as suicide bombers. What makes this shift particularly disturbing is that there seems to be a general belief, although inaccurate, that women are unlikely to perform a suicide mission. This can lead to a false sense of security when in the company of women--a false sense of security that can be lethal.

Another disturbing tactic is that of using children to perform suicide missions. I believe this is being used more and more because enemies of western culture believe that we will not engage a child in combat. Therefore, a child carrying a suicide bomb would have a much better chance of moving about undetected than an adult--particularly an adult male. This practice was also used during WWII as the German Army had a ready supply of children available in the form of the "Deutsches Jungvolk" or "Hitler Jugend" which were both forms of the Hitler Youth. The "Deutsches Jungvolk" was for young men ages 10-13 and the "Deutsches Jungvolk" was for young men from 13–18. The tactic worked for a short period of time; however, soon the allies realized that the children of the *Third Reich* were just as dangerous as their parents and treated them as such.

But regardless of whether a suicide bomber is a male, female, adult or child, perhaps the most frightening aspect of this type of attack is the mindset required to carry it out. In order for a person to strap explosives to themselves, enter a location and detonate the device, that individual must possess an extraordinary degree of fanaticism--one which most Americans find, frankly, inconceivable. It is this mental behavior which makes these individuals even more dangerous and more terrifying than the act itself; for they have no fear of death, and therefore have absolutely nothing to loose.

Vehicle bombs—This type of bombing is extremely common in Iraq and throughout the Middle East but is relatively rare in the United States. Car bombs, as they are now commonly called, involve packing a vehicle with explosives and using it to create damage and destruction to hard targets such as buildings. They are also used to create ambushes, road blocks and distractions. This type of attack may also involve a suicide bomber, but not always, as a car bomb can be rigged to detonate from a distance.

Simultaneous bombings—This type of attack is actually a series of attacks which are all carried out at the same time, but in different locations. Recently, we have seen this type of attack most often in Iraq. While rare, simultaneous bombings create an extremely elevated level of fear in the general population in or near the attack sites, in addition to causing the usual concern over the damage done by the actual explosives. Here is one example of what we mean by simultaneous bombings:

April 3, 2005—A bomb exploded in Southern Thailand's Hat Yai International airport, killing two people. It was followed, almost immediately, by another detonation which occurred in front of a Hat Yai hotel. Within moments, a third bomb exploded outside of a French-owned market a few miles North of Hat Yai. It was reported that all three devices were remotely detonated by cellular telephones. As a result of this attack, more than 54 people were injured. While I cannot tell you how to prevent an attack of this type, I can tell you that those who maintain self-control and composure during an attack will generally manage best.

Weapons of mass destruction—Until recent times, weapons of mass destruction (WMDs) were used only in reference to nuclear missiles owned and controlled by foreign nations. Since 9/11 however, the fear regarding the potential use of these devices, by rogue nations or terrorists, has increased exponentially. In addition, there are a number of WMDs sub-categories that we now need to be aware of. While the general populace is neither prepared nor equipped to deal with countering a threat resulting from the use of WMDs, there are things you can, and should do, in the event of such an attack that will better insure your ability to survive.

In this section, we will begin with a cursory overview of the types of attacks which you may encounter.

Biological Weapons—Perhaps one of the most insidious forms of terrorism involves the use of biological weapons. The reason this method of terrorism is so insidious is because often the victims will not realize they have been attacked until symptoms appear. And the time it takes for this to happen depends on a number of factors, including the length of time the victim was exposed, the concentration of the agent used and the general health of the victim. In fact, the use of biological contaminants dates back to the middle-ages and possibly even earlier, when plague-infected corpses were launched from catapults over castle walls. When the opposing army came in contact with the corpses, infection and disease would begin to spread. Another example of early biological warfare was applied by the U.S. Military during the Indian wars. Smallpox infected blankets were sometimes be given to or traded with the Indians, causing the deadly disease to spread throughout the tribe.

More recently, the U.S. experienced a biological attack which involved the use of anthrax spores being mailed to selected individuals. When the recipients opened the letters, they became exposed to the disease. Several people became ill and some subsequently died as a result of their exposure.

Some of the symptoms of exposure to biological contaminants include the following:

- Flu-like symptoms
- Fatigue and/or exhaustion,
- Rapid weight loss
- Stomach Pain
- Diarrhea
- Dyspnea (difficulty breathing)
- Respiratory Failure

However it must be remembered that each agent will have different effects, and as a result, there is no hard and fast rule for indicating exposure outside of medical testing.

Chemical Weapons—The effects of chemical weapons can be just as deadly as biological agents and are classified into four separate groups: nerve, blood, blister and incapacitating agents.

With the use of a chemical agent you will generally feel the effects immediately. The symptoms of exposure depend largely on the type of agent used, and can include the following:

- Burning or blistering of the skin and eyes
- Violent coughing
- Dizziness
- Nausea
- Fatigue
- Headache
- Convulsions
- Involuntary evacuation of the bowels and/or bladder

Other indicators of a possible chemical attack include signs that you may be aware of, but which are not directly related to your own condition. Examples of these might be the observance of numerous dead insects and animals in a given area, mass panic around you, oily droplets or film on the surface of objects, unusual odors and discoloration or other unexplained changes in surrounding plant life.

Radioactive ("Dirty") Bombs—Another frequently used buzz word is "dirty bomb." If we listen to mass media it's easy to assume this type of attack would leave the kind of widespread destruction that resulted from the bombings of Hiroshima or Nagasaki.

However, the truth is that a *dirty bomb* is actually nothing more than a conventional explosive that has been wrapped around radioactive material.

When the device is detonated, the contaminated material spreads. While the actual detonation does cause physical damage, the *dirty bomb* is typically used by terrorists more for the panic and terror it will creates than for the actual, physical damage it will cause.

Steps you can take

The types of threats mentioned, above, have been added solely to make you more aware of what is possible in our world today. In reality, there is little that can be done by the average citizen to counter an attack with a WMD, biological/chemical agent or a *dirty bomb,* with the exception of being aware of your immediate surroundings (situational awareness) and being prepared both mentally and physically to retreat to a safer location and advise the proper authorities.

The only possible exception to this would be if you were confronted with an assault by a suicide bomber or a mass shooter, whom you are able to correctly identify as such. In such cases, you would need to be properly trained to effectively determine the nature of, and engage in preventing, this type of threat.

While you might think it would be obvious if an individual were a mass shooter, recognizing a danger is very different from having the correct mindset and tactical ability to engage and counter such a threat effectively. It is recommended, therefore, that if you do not possess the specialized training or skills necessary to successfully counter such an attack, you make every effort to retreat from such attack. It must also be remembered that there is no disgrace in retreating from a situation which you have no means of winning or effectively countering, and your actions immediately following an attack of this type can mean the difference between life and death for not only yourself but others as well. Remember this phrase "Retreat today to live and fight another day."

In conclusion

While many people would rather walk around in a state of denial espousing the line "It will never happen here," they are wrong! All one has to do is watch the television every day to see that the level of attacks being engaged in by fanatical terrorists are on the rise.

Although several European countries have their own homegrown militants, we must be particularly wary of the militant Middle Eastern factions that appear to be testing their methods overseas, in an effort to see what works and what does not, before attempting further attacks on American soil. In Spain, for example, there was a recent detonation of an apartment complex by alleged members of al-Qaeda; the British police found the biological agent, Ricin, in a London flat, presumably part of a plan to release the biological agent in a terror attack. And let's not forget the tragic scenario that unfolded with the attack on the school in Basra where over 300 children were killed by Muslim extremists.

Domestic terrorism and related criminal acts

In the first part of this section we dealt mainly with acts of terrorism which are conducted by foreign enemies. But as we touched on, briefly, these are not the only type of terrorists which exist. Right here in the United States we have our own homegrown variety of terrorist. In addition to individuals bent of wreaking havoc, like the young boys who were responsible for the Columbine tragedy, there are other groups we must be watchful for. These are members of radical environmentalist and/or activist groups; and while they rarely target individuals, they can be extremely destructive when their energies are used to target property. What's more, there is always the possibility of inadvertent loss of life, even if one's goal is simply to cause the destruction of a building or vehicle. However, generally speaking, I do not consider them a *high level* threat provided their targets are property as opposed to people.

Conversely, there are some radical activist groups, such as pro-life activists, who use their radical religious beliefs to justify targeting abortion clinics and sometimes physicians. These are people who murder in the name of preserving life. While the issue of abortion itself is not the topic of this section, the perpetrators of such crimes do cross the line when they use acts of violence to express their position. The reason their actions are classified as domestic terrorism is because the intent behind the attacks is to intimidate other physicians into refusing to performing this legal medical procedure. Remember, terrorism implies more than violence, it implies violence with an intent to influence, manipulate or otherwise coerce others into thinking or behaving in a way that is consistent with the perpetrator.

Up to now, we have discussed what is referred to as single-issue terrorism, meaning terrorism which an individual or group commits against an individual or entity for a single, generally political, purpose.

Now, however, we will branch out and discuss other types of violent crime, which are more common here in the U.S.

When the word *terrorism* is heard, most people envision images of car bombs, political assassinations, kidnappings, masked attackers, and the like. However, for decades the citizens of this country have been terrorized by a domestic form of terrorism, one that is often not reported to the authorities and is even less frequently reported in the media.

While the official FBI definition of terrorism is "the unlawful use of force or violence against persons or property to intimidate or coerce a government, the civilian population, or any segment thereof, in furtherance of political or social objectives," an easier definition might be "any act of violence or threat of violence against a person or property for the purpose of obtaining an individual or group goal or objective." In this sense, we would not only include the likes of the Columbine shooting or the more recent mass murders at Red Lake High School in our broadened definition of domestic terrorism; but we would also need to include other crimes (such as certain forms of stalking) which either are or maintain the potential to become violent crimes committed specifically to gain control or otherwise manipulate, using violence or the threat of violence.

Stalking:

In this section we will be discussing one of the most insidious forms of domestic terrorism: stalking. While some may not consider stalking to be a form of domestic terrorism, it is my belief, based on the FBI definition of terrorism, that stalking must be included. While the stalker's goal, as we will see later, is usually a social rather than a political one, the stalker within certain cases will use the threat of force or violence, in order to sway the opinion or actions of their victim. In addition, stalking typically includes an invasion of the victim's personal privacy, the general feeling of powerlessness on the part of the victim, and a persistent feeling of fear or terror. What's more, a stalking scenario can take place over a prolonged period of time, making it not only insidious but downright debilitating as well.

While many associate stalking with celebrities and other VIPs, anyone can become the victim of a stalker. According to a 1997 U.S. department of justice study, there are currently between 20,000 and 2 million stalkers in the United States alone. The report further indicates, that on average, one in twelve women are stalked at some point in their life. What's more, a woman is three times more likely to be stalked than raped. In fact, the chances of being stalked are close to one in ten; approximately 80% of stalking victims are women and of that 80%, approximately 8% are under the age of eighteen.

However women are not the only targets of stalkers. Each year close to 1,007,000 women and over 380,000 men are stalked in the United States. Yet, according to statistics, approximately 50% of these victims will never report the crime. And of the 50% that do file a police report, it is estimated that only one-quarter of them ever obtain a restraining order against their stalker. Unfortunately, this may be due in part to the fact that a restraining order offers little or no real protection from an assailant. This is because approximately 80% of restraining orders are violated.

Therefore a restraining order may often only serve elevate the activity level and aggression of the stalker towards their victim.

What are we dealing with?

As with all other forms of self-defense, before one can engage an enemy, it is imperative to first understand that enemy. In this section we will briefly discuss the motivation, mindset and methodology of the stalker. But first, we define what stalking is. Generally, stalking is the overly persistent and an unwanted pursuit of, or level of obsessive harassment against, one person toward another, causing the victim to be fearful of potential bodily harm or injury.

Stalking can manifest in several ways, some of which begin with what appear to be very benign actions. For example, in the case of celebrities, repeated gifts and/or letters intended to be signs of the stalker's affection can, on occasion, lead to more serious consequences. This can happen due to the psychosis of the stalker which renders him/her unable to accept rejection, or lack of reciprocation of feelings, on the part of the victim. On occasion, a deep resentment develops which can lead to violence, not only against the victim, but against third parties such as the victim's family members and/or friends whom the stalker may perceive as impeding the stalker's progress. Now let's examine the four types of stalker obsessions and the psychological causes for their behavior.

1. *Simple obsessional*—This type of stalking tends to occur when the victim and the stalker have actually met or have some knowledge of one another. The simple obsessional pathology is considered by many to be one the most dangerous types of obsession. While the psychological reasons for it are too complicated to go into here, the more common manifestations of this type of stalking include the desire for vengeance and/or an attempt to use intimidation to coerce the victim into entering into a new intimate relationship or reviving a previous one.

2. *Love obsessional*—This type of obsession is often characterized by the absence of an existing relationship between the victim and the stalker. In most cases, the victims are known to the stalker through either the media or some other form of public venue. This type of obsession can occur to non-celebrities as well, although a significant number of stalkers who engage in the *love obsessional* pathology tend to focus on celebrities or other public figures. Stalkers in this category often suffer from a mental disorder such as bipolar disorder or schizophrenia. Quite often they have never been involved in a serious personal relationship themselves, and therefore they believe that if only they can make themselves known to the object of their affections, the emotions they feel will be reciprocated. This is usually done in the form of letters sent to the victim. Due to the psychological pathology suffered by the stalker, quite often the messages contained in these letters will be disturbing enough to create a sense of intimidation or fear in the victim. Naturally, the recipient of such attentions would not be inclined to respond; and yet, the failure of the victim to respond to such messages often leads to increased frustration on the part of the stalker, which may cause them to increase their efforts to gain their victim's attention. This may also lead to the use of other methods to make that connection. In this scenario, a long-term management approach is often required to prevent the obsession from escalating beyond simple written communication. While the danger of physical harm in such a scenario is considered less than in the case of the simple obsessional pathology, monitoring is nevertheless recommended.

3. *Erotomania*—*Erotomanic* behaviors are distinct and different from *love obsessional* behaviors, in that the *erotomanic* stalker actually believes the victim is in love with him/her while the *love obsessional* stalker makes it a goal to make the victim fall in love with him/her.

Another significant and unique quality of the *erotomanic* stalker is that frequently the stalker will be female and the victim male. In addition, the male victims in such cases are often older and of a higher socioeconomic class than the stalker. Although this type of behavior can result in extremely aggressive behavior on the part of the stalker, research has shown that these types of stalkers do not, generally, present a significant danger of physical harm to their victims. This assumption, however, should not be considered an absolute, as several variables can alter the behavior of a stalker with this form of pathology. And in extreme cases, *erotomanic* stalkers do commit violence. When this happens it is usually with the justification that, if they cannot have the victim, no one else will either.

4. *False victimization syndrome*—The fourth and final behavior or obsessive type is marked by a desire on the part of the stalker to control another by obtaining sympathy. A vast majority of those with this pathology are female. The underlying psychological pathology accompanying this behavior is *narcissism*. The way this tends to manifest is that the stalker will develop the desire to be the sole focus of the victim. While this form of obsession can be physically dangerous, performing acts of violence that result in physical injury to the victim will usually only occur to the stalker if they believe it will allow them to gain the sympathy of their victim or will enable them to present a more convincing argument to the victim.

I would like to emphasize that the preceding classifications of stalkers provide a very general overview only. It must be remembered that the underlying psychological conditions and pathologies which lead to stalking behavior are vast and complicated. The information above is presented with only one purpose in mind: to help you better understand an enemy I hope you will never encounter.

Before we move on to the next section, I've got another story for you. The following is an actual account of a case which directly impacted several people's lives, including my own. As the story unfolds, take special note of the warning signs of stalking, as outlined above.

Several years ago, a long-time friend of mine, whom I have known since I was a teenager, became romantically involved with a woman he met at a social function. This woman doggedly pursued my friend. She repeatedly wrote letters to him and left voice messages for him. I had the opportunity to listen to many of these messages. While my friend believed her messages did not convey anything more than a sincere desire to maintain his interest, I believed that they indicated a psychological problem and I warned him about it. Unfortunately, he did not heed my warning.

Shortly after their relationship began, my friend (we will call him "John") decided to withdraw from the social group that he and this woman had both been part of. I remember when this happened because I had stopped by his house and he asked me to listen to the message on his answering machine left by this woman, whom we will call "Jean." The message was, for the most part, a continuous rambling of largely unintelligible speech, but what could be heard and understood was that she could not go on without John as part of the group, and that she would *die* if he did not return.

Now, John is a very sensitive and gentle man, and this caused him a great deal of concern. While he did not return to the group, he began to see more of Jean. I told him at the time that I felt there was something wrong with her. Unfortunately, my concerns were again ignored and their relationship grew. Initially, things between them seemed quite good. John's spirits seemed high and there did not appear to be anything other than the usual relationship problems which occurred from time to time.

But at some point, I do not remember exactly when, Jean began to become very possessive of John. This led to an obsessive level of concern over another of John's female friends. While he had no romantic involvement with this other woman whom we will call "Betty," Jean began to accuse John of seeing Betty behind Jean's back. At first, John considered the behavior to be indicative of nothing more than typical female jealousy. I, however, began to observe the development of a more disconcerting pattern. Over the next few years, I observed a number of disturbing events. I discovered that Jean was in the habit of checking John's mailbox when he was not home. On one occasion I confronted her about it and she said that she was looking for "love letters" from Betty. I knew that John and Betty did not have a romantic relationship, and I expressed my concerns to John, but as before, they were ignored. At one point I told John that I was becoming increasingly concerned over the level of jealousy I could see developing, and even joked half-heartedly that he should be careful that he does not come home and find a "rabbit boiling in the pot" (referring to a scene in the movie *Fatal Attraction*). Had I known then what was to happen, I would have pressed him even harder. But at the time I told myself that John was a grown man and was quite capable of taking care of himself, although I did continually warn him that Jean was unstable and was not only obsessed with Betty, but that she also perceived me as a threat.

I came to this conclusion based on a number of behaviors, some of which are outlined below. During the course of Jean and John's relationship, Jean demanded that John to stop going to his favorite coffee shop, demanded that he tell her where he was going whenever he left the house, required him to call her as soon as he returned and made a variety of accusations against me, including that I was planning to put a lien against his property for back taxes and throw him out on the street. Jean also accused me of covering for John so that he could see Betty.

I suspect she began to target me more aggressively because of the closeness of my relationship with John, and this was something that obviously threatened her. Also, I had (on several occasions) suggested that she seek professional help. But Jean realized that John would always seek to avoid any kind of conflict. In fact, often he would simply stop doing what he enjoyed just to keep Jean from accusing him of something he'd have to defend against later. It is likely that she felt this same tactic would work to separate me from John. However, her accusations against me failed to have the desired effect, and my relationship with John continued.

One night, when my wife and I returned home after an evening out, I observed someone walking around on my front porch. I exited my vehicle, and approached the individual. It was Jean. She said that I needed to come to John's house with her, as she had not heard from or seen him in a few days. Upon arrival at his house, which was only about a block away, we observed that there were no lights on and that his car was still in the driveway. This was unusual because although he did not often go out at night, he generally would stay up to watch TV. After knocking and repeatedly ringing the doorbell without any response, I prepared to kick in the door when Jean pulled out a key.

She opened the door, and we entered John's house. I called out to John, but received no response, so I continued to search the first floor. I remember entering the bathroom and seeing the shower doors closed and thinking to myself: *please do not let there be a body in here.* (I had seen too many cases where people had slipped in the shower and were found days later). I opened the shower and it was empty. I then searched the back pantry of the house and also found nothing. Next I heard Jean call to me. I returned to the front foyer, and she said "he is upstairs." On my way to the stairs I asked if she had already gone upstairs, and she said "no." As I reached the top of the stairs I began to get an uneasy feeling and knew something was very wrong. I searched the first two rooms with no luck, then entered the third and final room.

When I turned on the light, I observed a sickening scene. John was lying on the bed, unresponsive, with his eyes rolled back in his head. There was blood, urine, and fecal matter all over the place. His breathing was extremely shallow and labored, and he did not have any detectable extremity pulses. I checked his carotid pulse (in his neck), and found that it was weak to the point of almost being non-existent. I immediately called out to Jean and my wife, telling them to call 911 and report a possible stroke.

I followed the ambulance to the hospital and after John was admitted I spoke with the treating physician, who said that it was extremely unlikely he would survive the next few hours. However John managed to stabilize, although he was in a coma.

I spoke with the treating physician in the intensive care unit and he asked me if it was possible that John had ingested anything. I told him that based upon his religious beliefs, I did not think it possible that he did so intentionally, however I promised that I would search his house to see what I could find. John's niece and I arrived at the house and began our search. At first, nothing was found that would indicate anything out of the ordinary. Then I entered the pantry and discovered an open box of rat poison. I made a mental note of this, and continued the search without finding anything else. When I spoke with the doctor again, I informed him of my findings. He told me that rat poison (as I already knew) contained strychnine and that John's illness (which was diagnosed as *acute idiopathic renal failure*) was consistent with strychnine poisoning. Blood tests were ordered, however the results were returned inconclusive.

At no time over the next several days did Jean even make an appearance at the hospital. John's niece (whom I contacted) and I maintained a constant vigil. During the following two weeks, while John was hooked up to a respirator, we did not leave him alone for more than 10-15 minutes at a time, and even during these times we made sure a nurse was with him. John came out of his coma approximately two weeks after I had found him, and once strong enough I asked him about the rat poison. He said that he had not had any problems with mice or rats since 1968, and that was the last time he bought any rat poison. He was confused as to why a new box was in his house. I asked him if Jean had been cooking for him, and he told me she had. This caused me great concern. I discussed the situation with John's niece and we decided to take some preventive measures, which included restricting unsupervised visits to those of whom we approved. The doctors agreed, and Jean was at the top of the restricted list. Once she learned that she could not visit John without either myself or John's niece being present, she became enraged, and accused both of us of stealing from John. The accusations were, of course, groundless. But this shows the extent to which a delusional person will go when threatened with exposure.

Once John was released from the hospital he parted ways with Jean. Betty has since died, and life has returned to some level of normalcy, but John suffered permanent kidney damage from his ordeal and is still required to receive dialysis three times per week.

While I cannot prove it, I believe Jean poisoned John in an effort to either control him by requiring increased assistance from her, or perhaps even to kill him because in her pathological state she thought that if she could not have him no one else should either.

This is just one example of how a series of pathological behaviors can factor into a stalking scenario, and it shows how stalking behavior can begin, develop, and end in a life or death situation if caution is not maintained.

Identifying a stalker

The behavior referred to as *stalking* has been a part of the human psyche since recorded history, as is evident, for example, in Shakespeare's play *Othello*. Although, until approximately 1990, the act of stalking was not even considered a crime. However, in light of some of the tragic events, which befell some prominent people as a result of this type of behavior, such as the murder of John Lennon and the much publicized shooting of Ronald Reagan by a Jodie Foster fanatic, virtually every state in the country has since enacted some form of anti-stalking law. In fact, today the act of stalking is treated as seriously as rape, assault and murder. It is for these reasons that the comparison between terrorism and stalking can be made. The only real difference between them is that in the case of terrorism, the intended victim is society and in the case of stalking, the intended victim is an individual. However, the ultimate goal of both terrorism and stalking is to change the behavior or thinking of the victim to match that of the attacker.

So to begin this section on identifying a stalker, we must first acknowledge that it is almost impossible to identify a potential stalker until the activities associated with the act of stalking begin. The following is a list of characteristics commonly found in stalkers.

☐ Most, but certainly not all, stalkers are male. There are documented cases of female stalkers such as the woman who believed that she was married to David Letterman. But generally speaking, this particular form of domestic terrorism is committed by men.

☐ While not always the case, there is an increased likelihood that the stalker has a history of either sub-stance abuse, psychiatric illness or criminal behavior.

☐ A stalker will usually have higher overall intelligence than other types of criminals.

Stalking behavior

As mentioned in the preceding paragraphs, it is virtually impossible to know if somebody is planning to be a stalker. The real key is when the stalking behavior begins. The following is a list of stalking behaviors to watch out for.

- *Persistent telephone calls*—By persistent I mean regular, consistent calls, which continue despite instructions to the caller, from either the authorities or the victim, to cease all forms of contact.

- *Lying in wait*—Waiting at the workplace or within the victim's neighborhood or any other areas where the stalker would otherwise have no reason to be.

- *Making threats*—Direct threats that are made either in writing, or over the telephone. Also included in this category are indirect threatening behaviors like leaving a dead animal for the victim to find or sending dead flowers.

- *Manipulation*—Manipulative behaviors include threatening to commit suicide or perform some other action that is designed to illicit a sympathetic response from, or to initiate contact with, the victim.

- *Delusional romantic gestures*—Otherwise non-threatening letters, e-mails, gifts or other forms of communication (such as graffiti) that suggest that a romantic scenario exists between the stalker and the victim.

- *Rumor mongering*—Character defamation may be used by a stalker to blackmail the victim into performing according to the stalker's will. Common examples of this would include spreading rumors of infidelity or other inappropriate behaviors.

- *Victim objectification*—Objectifying or dehumanizing the victim allows the stalker to act out against the victim without the usual sense of remorse, guilt, or empathy.

- *Violation of privacy*—Photographing or video taping the victim without his/her consent is a violation of personal privacy that is often associated with stalking.

What can be done?

In this section we will discuss some general guidelines for dealing with stalkers.

Physical defense against a stalker is actually no different from the physical defense that would be used against any other type of assailant. The key is to first do everything possible to avoid a violent confrontation with the individual. However, when all other alternatives have been exhausted and the victim is confronted by an imminent attack, the only remaining counter measure is one of immediate aggressive violence, on the part of the victim, against the stalker.

While these words may seem strong, due to the psychological condition of the attacker, the potential for rational discussion once the situation has developed to the point of imminent violence, is highly unlikely. For this reason, victims must treat their stalker as they would any other criminal who would seek to do them harm. This brings us to the issue of firearms.

It is not uncommon for a victim of a stalker to seek to obtain a firearm for personal defense; however, in some cases this action can be significantly more dangerous than remaining unarmed. Whereas, I strongly advocate the use of private firearms for the purpose of self-protection, I also believe that anyone who seeks to utilize a firearm for any purpose, should first undergo extensive training. One reason such training is necessary is that there is no such thing as a routine attack. Emotions and individual personalities play a factor in how we deal with violent confrontations. In addition, an individual will react differently when confronted with a spontaneous act of violence as opposed to one that has developed over time as the result of harassment by a stalker. In the latter case, there will likely be an increased level of anxiety, fear, and resentment due to the fact that the situation has been escalating over a period of time.

Therefore, I would recommend that any victim of a stalker

who wishes to purchase a firearm for defense, seek out professional training and guidance from a competent and qualified instructor. This is often the best alternative for protecting the individual against an attack. However, many people do not have the financial resources to hire a security professional and are thus required to either rely on the police or their own wits, skill and training, for their personal defense.

As I mentioned earlier, there are several things the victim can do before seeking to arm him/herself. For instance, you can start by filing a written police report or statement outlining your situation as a victim of a stalker. You may also petition the court for a restraining order against the individual. But as I also mentioned, these actions will not protect you from aggression by the stalker. And in some cases, they will only add to the anger and frustration felt by the stalker, which may increase the chances of violence on their part.

So here are six steps you can take to properly protect yourself, short of arming yourself and paying an instructor or consultant for professional training. These steps will not only help to protect you from a physical attack, but they will also protect you from potential criminal liability that can result from a situation in which you are forced to use violence against a stalker in self-defense.

1. *Talk about it.* If you are, or suspect you might be, the victim of a stalker, advise friends, family and neighbors of the situation and do not deny that it is happening. This must be done so that the people who surround you on a daily basis can be additional eyes and ears for you. It is also important because that can later serve as witnesses to your legitimate concerns for your own personal safety.

2. *Ignore the stalker.* Do not, under any circumstances, attempt to communicate, rationalize, deal or otherwise negotiate with a stalker. A stalker is not a rational person and any attempt to communicate on your part will only

serve to validate their delusions and create a feeling of enablement on their part.

3. *Document everything.* Always document and report any incident to the police, regardless of how insignificant it may appear at the time. As we saw with Jean and John, a situation that begins as a *normal* one can quickly become something else. It is extremely important to have a complete record of ongoing harassment, which will assist you greatly should the final result of the stalking situation be one that involves physical violence.

4. *Attempt normalcy.* While this may seem difficult, if not impossible, try to make every effort to live your life with as little disruption as possible. That said, it must also be said that you must increase your situational awareness to be prepared for anything that might arise. Refer to the tips for improving situational awareness in the beginning of this book for assistance with that and remember that practicing these techniques now will make it that much easier to put them to use if you should need them later.

5. *Change your contact information.* In extreme cases it may be necessary to change your phone number, move and/or obtain a P.O. box for your mail. If you do need to take such measures, be sure to use a commercial P. O. box rather than one supplied through the U.S. Post Office. The reason for this, is that private companies make it harder for unauthorized personnel to obtain the box holder's information.

6. *Win at all costs.* If a violent confrontation occurs, do not forget that you are the victim and that you are fighting for your life. Do not allow misplaced sympathy/concern for the stalker or fear of legal ramifications to prevent you from taking the action necessary to win, and win at all costs.

The steps outlined above are only a starting point. If you wish to build on this knowledge, I recommend picking up a copy of *The Psychology of Stalking,* by J. Reid Meloy. It is an excellent source for additional information on this complicated topic.

Carjacking:

The U.S. Department of Justice defines carjacking as the violent theft of an occupied motor vehicle. According to a U.S. Government report, released in March of 1999, approximately 49,000 carjackings took place annually, between 1992 and 1996. These figures were up from earlier estimates of about 35,000/year during the period from 1987 to 1992. The latest reports show that carjackings grew from 3% of all motor vehicle thefts in 1992 to 3.5% in 1996. In about 90% of completed carjackings, weapons were used and in about 70% of those carjackings the weapon was a firearm. However, only 23% of completed carjackings and 10% of failed carjacking attempts, resulted in injuries. Ninety-two% of all carjacking incidents involved a lone victim; men were more likely than women to be the victimized; and urban residents were more likely than suburban or rural residents to be carjacked.

35% of completed carjackings were reported to insurers. A study by the Illinois State Police covering 1994 to 1996 found that most of the 45 carjackings it studied, 60% of the perpetrators involved had known gang affiliations. Their primary motivation appeared to be a need for short-term transportation.

The Anti-Car Theft Act, which became law in 1992, was designed to reduce the number of car thefts nationwide and make armed auto theft (aka: carjacking) a federal crime. In 1994, the passage of the *Violent Crime Control and Law Enforcement Act* made carjackings resulting in death a federal crime punishable by death.

Methods for preventing and/or mitigating a carjacking

The following methods and principles can be applied by anyone who drives, to help to prevent (or at least minimize) the chances of becoming a carjacking victim. They include actions to take both before and during a carjacking:

☐ Always be concerned about your personal safety first. The vehicle can be replaced, you cannot.

☐ Make yourself as hard a target as possible. In other words, let your actions and behaviors be such a potential hazard or burden to the carjacker that he will seek out an easier victim. To begin with, always be situationally aware of your surroundings. Always park in well lit areas. If something looks suspicious, do not approach the vehicle.

☐ Always avoid secluded areas of a parking lot or car park. When in a commuter parking garage, always try to park close to the openings to the street. The reason, is that should an incident occur, it will be easier to yell for help.

☐ Never be afraid to drop your packages or keys and flee the area; as generally, the carjacker is more interested in the car than you and will likely not try to pursue you.

☐ When stopped in traffic, maintain a minimum distance of one car length between yourself and the vehicle in front of you, as this will allow for greater maneuverability in the event of a dangerous situation.

☐ While driving or stopped, always keep your doors locked, and whenever possible your windows up. If you do choose to roll your windows down, you will need to be more situationally aware to the activity around you.

☐ If you are stopped by a police officer, lock your doors and only open the window enough to communicate with the officer. If you feel any concern or suspect that something is amiss you can request the officer to request a second patrol car. This will ensure that you are dealing with legitimate police personnel. (The reason for this action is that a relatively new technique of some criminals is to pose as the police and pull over motorists with flashing lights. Once stopped, the victims are at the mercy of the phony police and are susceptible to rape, carjackings and assault or worse).

While the preceding list is not all-inclusive, the points outlined should help to offset the potential for this type of attack.

For further clarification, here is an example of what I would call *suspicious* behaviors. One holiday season a rumor was going around that thieves were hiding under cars so that when people exited the mall with their Christmas gifts, the thieves would attack at the most opportune instant, which would generally be while the shopper was attempting to unlock his/her car door. Because it was Christmas and I had one last gift to purchase for a client, I decided that I would make a very quick stop at the mall. I had one of my dogs (an Akita) with me and because I was only going to be gone for a few minutes and the weather was mild (around 50°), I allowed her to stay in the vehicle. When I returned to my vehicle I was not very concerned at first. But as I approached the vehicle my dog was hysterical. This was a definite sign that something was wrong. I immediately became more alert as I prepared for a potential confrontation.

As I approached the vehicle I made it a point to look around the entire vehicle. I looked underneath as well, but found nothing alarming. I proceeded to insert the key in the lock. The dog was still very upset. As I turned to see what she was barking at, I observed two young men dressed in heavy down coats with their hands in their pockets. By this point, the dog was so agitated I thought she was going to break through the glass. This was actually a bit out of character for her, and this served to raise my concerns even higher. One of them said "Hey man, you got any money?" Now, those who know me will tell you that I am not intimidated easily, but this question was coupled with the observation that both of these boys (they didn't appear to be more than 15 or 16) had continued to keep their hands in their pockets and this served to make me even more suspicious because, as I said earlier, it was a relatively warm day. My response to them was "Yea, I have lots of money," to which they responded with "Well, why don't you give it to us?"

Understand that this is not a response I would advocate others use in response to such a question; however, I realized at this point that I was in a high degree of danger from these two and as such, I reacted accordingly. I raised my hands, and said "Look, I don't want any trouble." I then feigned reaching for my wallet, and instead drew my handgun and presented it to them muzzle first. Now, I had absolutely no desire to shoot either of them; however, I was fully prepared to do so if they moved in any way that I deemed was threatening to my safety. After I did this, they both removed their hands from their pockets, and raised them over their heads. Fortunately, mall security was patrolling the area as this occurred, and I was able to signal them as they passed. They contacted the local police, and upon their arrival, the matter was resolved without further incident. In the end, it was determined that these two punks did not have any weapons on them; however, I did not know this at the time and was not about to take a chance.

In this case, I had followed virtually all of the necessary steps to avoid this type of situation. In the end, it all came down to being situationally aware and to heeding the prior warning provided by my beloved dog. Thank you Tedra.

Here is another example of why situational awareness and willingness to act quickly and decisively is so important. The following story involves a young man whose parents hired me to train him in firearms safety. One summer day, while on my way to my girlfriend's house, I stopped at the drive-through of a local fast food restaurant. After placing my order, I pulled up toward the pick-up window and I observed a great deal of activity occurring in the front of the restaurant. There were people all over the place--it looked like they were having a party. I did not think much about it, and continued to the window. As I was advancing toward the exit, I was stopped in line because of traffic. While seated, I continued to look around me as I always do, and out of my blind spot someone approached my vehicle. My window was still down. I immediately felt something poking into my chest as I heard the words "Hey mister, give me your money." My immediate reaction was to look down at my chest, which I did, as my support side hand moved in that direction, and my master hand moved for my weapon. Fortunately, when I looked down, I did not see a weapon in my attacker's hand. My support hand then grabbed the wrist of my attacker, and applied a reverse wrist-lock which caused the attacker's arm to be twisted away from me and his head to strike my mirror. My master hand then came around and struck the attacker in the face two or three times with a technique known as a heel strike. I then exited my vehicle, while still maintaining my hold on the attacker through the window, and that is when I identified him: it was my young student! After the requisite yelling, I told him to get in the truck as I was taking him back to his parents. On the way, I asked him what he was thinking, and his reply was "I was just screwing around." I told him as I told his parents, that he is extremely lucky that his "screwing around" did not get him killed.

Home invasions:

While home invasions are not considered a high frequency crime, these events do occur; and when they do, the psychological trauma that results can be extensive, as this form of attack tends to be extremely violent in nature. The sense of violation one will often feel can in some cases have a far reaching and lasting impact on the lives of the victims.

The reasons for such damaging psychological effects are clear from the case of a man who contacted me about training immediately following a home invasion and attack which targeted his family. I had read about the incident in the local newspaper, which described how two attackers had forced their way into the home of this individual and restrained all of the occupants, including his daughter, his son, and the wife of the man who subsequently contacted me. The ordeal these people endured lasted several hours and culminated with the rape of both women (which the man was forced to watch) after which the man was forced to drive the attackers to an ATM, where he withdrew the maximum amount of cash allowed. After turning his cash over to the attackers, he was abandoned and his vehicle was stolen.

When he contacted me about training in the use of a weapon, I asked him as I do everyone, what his reason for seeking training was. He told me who he was and what had occurred. I could hear the anxiety and anger in his voice. He explained the entire story to me, much of which was not presented in the media, and expressed to me that he would never allow this to happen again. Ironically, prior to this incident, both he and his wife were adamantly against owning a firearm, but because of this violation, their positions had changed. It is truly a sad thing that a crime of this viciousness is often needed to make people aware of the responsibility they have for their own safety and security.

Methods for preventing and/or mitigating a home invasion

In addition to the standard preventive actions such as always locking the doors and windows at night, using solid core doors, checking before answering the door, installing panic alarms, etc., which will assist in the prevention of this type of attack, the importance of a plan of action to be taken in the event that a home invasion occurs while the residents are asleep is essential. Therefore, we will now discuss the development of such a plan. First, we will discuss what you should do when you think an invader may have entered your home, followed by what you shouldn't do.

When you were a child, your parents had a fire escape plan, right? This was so that if a fire ever broke out in your house, everyone would know what to do and where to meet. The same principles can be applied here. A family plan of action, for use when an intruder may be in your home, could mean the difference between life and death.

Create a safe room

A safe room is exactly as the name implies; it is a room in the house (usually the master bedroom) where the whole family can meet and lock the door if it is believed that an intruder has entered the premises. The importance of this technique can be seen in the following story which is an actual event and describes the wrong actions to take, followed by recommendations for the proper course of action.

A man and woman are in their home asleep when the woman hears a sound coming from downstairs. She immediately wakes up the man and tells him what she has heard and that he needs to investigate. Reluctantly, he gets out of bed and begins to head down the stairs. He stops at the bottom of the stairs and looks toward the kitchen. The house is dark, as he steps off the landing of the stairs facing the kitchen. He walks three feet toward the kitchen and the last sound he hears is the sound of the bullet, which kills him. The intruder, to this day, has not been apprehended.

This is a clear example of the importance of knowing not only what to do, but also what *not* to do. When a noise is heard in the middle of the night, it is a natural instinct for people to attempt to discover the cause of it. But as we can see from this story, the results can be tragic.

If this family had a safe room as well as a plan of action to fall back on during the above scenario, the man who was shot dead in his hallway, might be alive today.

Items to have in your safe room

Like any other activity, certain items are required to accomplish specific tasks. In the case of a home invasion, the items that you should have in your safe room include the following:

A cellular telephone—This is used to contact outside help in the event that the telephone lines leading to the house are damaged or cut. This may seem like the plot of a movie, but cutting of the phone lines prior to entering a home is becoming a more frequent technique of the home invader.

A sturdy lock on the door—A sturdy locking door on your safe room is essential to help slow down an attacker. Remember: to a criminal, time is a greater enemy than the police.

A firearm—This is controversial item and only the homeowner can make the decision as to whether to purchase a firearm. But if you do decide to use a firearm for home defense, a 12-gauge shotgun with 00 Buck 9 shot is the recommended choice. A handgun is also a viable option, but is considerably more restrictive in its application, due its single projectile and the need for greater accuracy--which, under stressful conditions may not be possible unless the user has received a significant amount of training.

A flashlight—This is used to not only monitor the interior of the room, but may also be used to identify the location of the attacker.

How to use your safe room

The way to use your safe room is to layout a plan and practice it with your family on a regular basis--monthly is good until everybody in the family knows what to do. Thereafter, practice your drill a minimum of every two months.

Once the plan has been made and practiced until it becomes natural, everyone in the family will know to meet in the safe room when it is believed that an intruder has entered the house. Once in this room, the following steps need to be taken:

Lock the door. Securely lock the door once all family members are safely inside the safe room.

Call 911. Using either the house telephone or the cellular telephone, dial 911, and provide the emergency services dispatcher with the following information:

- [ ] your name and address and the names of all family members in the safe room;

- [ ] the details of the situation that is occurring (i.e., an intruder is in the house);

- [ ] what you and the rest of you family are wearing as well as your exact location within the house (i.e., we are in a safe room located in the master bedroom on the west side of the house on the second floor);

- [ ] whether or not you are armed.

Some of this information may be written down ahead of time, such as the exact location of the safe room within the house, so that when your call is made there is more routine and less thinking to do.

Stay on the telephone with the dispatcher. Do this under all circumstances, regardless of what else happens, until the dispatcher advises you that the police are outside of the safe room door.

Your best chance for avoiding violence during a home invasion is to stay together in one place. If the intruder attempts to enter your safe room, advise him in no uncertain terms that you are armed (if true), the police have been notified, and that if he enters the room you will defend yourselves. All of this should be said loudly enough so that the police dispatcher can hear what you are saying. Emergency telephone lines are all recorded, and in the event that the intruder attempts to enter the safe room and you are forced to engage, this tape will serve as evidence that you did everything in your power to avoid a confrontation.

What not to do

We've all seen Hollywood movies where the victim searches the house, finds the intruder and shoots the bad guy. Unfortunately, that's Hollywood, not real life. As we saw in our previous example, attempting to engage an intruder is not a good idea. There are many more reasons for this than we have time to go into here, but the main one is this: the intruder knows where he is and has a reasonable idea where you are, but you have no idea where he is. This means that while you are searching for him, he may simply be waiting for you.

Even if you have been trained in the use of firearms, unless you have also received professional training in how to properly conduct a home search, you are much better off waiting in the safe room for the police to arrive.

In conclusion

It is my firm belief that the protection and defense of this country and its citizens from terrorism, or any other type of crime, is a *dual* responsibility; one that must be shared *between* the government and the citizens. While the government should make every effort possible to prevent these large scale attacks and to create and enforce laws that discourage domestic terrorism and other violent crimes, it is also the responsibility of each citizen to seek to avoid a conflict or violent confrontation. And when confronted with such a scenario, as we have outlined in the preceding chapters, we must each be responsible for our own security and protection, and that means being prepared to win at all costs.

Nothing in this book is intended to imply that citizens should seek terrorists or other criminals with whom to engage, nor that we should forgo our civil liberties in the name of greater security, which does appear to have occurred to some degree since 9/11. It is important to remember the immortal words of Benjamin Franklin, "Those who would sacrifice liberty for security deserve neither." Yet, through a series of behavioral changes, we may become more aware of our surroundings and more alert to potential threats.

In addition to our willingness to counter violent threats, as warranted, it is also imperative that we report suspicious activities. In Israel, a country which deals with violent threats almost daily, there are hundreds of incidents which never make it to the news, involving Israeli citizens who have successfully thwarted attacks of one form or another. The key to the success Israelis have demonstrated in preventing these attacks is often simply their situational awareness and the knowledge that the threat exists. The same principles can and should be applied here in our country.

By understanding the enemy and the threat they represent, we stand a much better chance of avoiding violent attacks, whether they come from domestic criminals or international terrorists. And should a situation in which we find ourselves escalate into a violent encounter, our understanding of our enemy will provide us with an increased chance of controlling the confrontation. However, *none* of this is possible without the necessary training and mental conditioning.

THE COLOR CODE ALERT SYSTEM

There are a number of aspects to the combat mindset. The combat mindset is really all about being mentally prepared to engage your attacker. As I have mentioned throughout this book, the decision to engage should always be based on your personal threat assessment, which is dependent on your own ability to maintain a high level of situational awareness. I have also stressed, repeatedly, that whenever possible, you should avoid a violent conflict. However, there may be times when you are forced to deal with a violent encounter. Should this happen, you must be prepared to fight and *win*.

The combat mindset results from being properly trained to take aggressive action, when necessary, and to win at all costs. One of the tools we use in self-defense training, which assists us in understanding the combat mindset, is a color coding system not unlike that which is used by the federal government for announcing terrorist threat alerts. The difference, however, is that our system is for describing the level of situational awareness and readiness an individual maintains, dependent on his own personal threat assessment.

In this next section, I will describe the color coding system as it is used within potentially violent confrontations dealing with the combat mindset.

Color Code Awareness

In the aftermath of 11 September 2001 the U.S. Government created a new department known as *Homeland Security* and also implemented a *Color Code Alert System*. This new system was designed to provide immediate alerts to the general population in relation to the threats posed by al-Qaeda or other terrorist groups. This system of alertness, however, is not new. The original system was created by Lt. Col. Jeff Cooper (retired), and was designed for use within the realm of personal defense and security.

As I explained earlier, being aware of one's surroundings and the events unfolding is critical to avoiding a violent confrontation and staying safe; however, one's surroundings are not static and may change rapidly. While most of the time, the threat of attack is low, it is important to remember that a seemingly non-threatening encounter may become violent in a matter of seconds. It is the dynamic nature of events that makes the color code system important. If you were to consistently walk around in a constant state of heightened alert, expecting an attacker to jump out from behind every bush, it would quickly exhaust your energies, and it is quite likely that the stress would bring you down before an attacker would.

The solution to a constant state of hyper-awareness is to adjust your level of alertness (or combat readiness, to use the military terminology) to match the actual situation. To make this match, it's important to consider the various levels of awareness and how they are determined. We will begin this next section, by listing the four levels of the *Color Code Alert System*.

Condition White

The lowest level of awareness one can be in is *Condition White*. In this condition you are almost completely unaware of what's going on around you and are not prepared to deal with any kind of conflict, threat or confrontation. Perhaps you're tired or worried about work or school. Perhaps alcohol or drugs have impaired your senses. Either way, in *Condition White*, you are not ready for anything and, in the event of an attack, the odds are stacked heavily against you.

Condition Yellow

In *Condition Yellow*, you are more alert but still relatively calm and relaxed. You scan your surroundings for threats or anything else out of the ordinary, but without the intense pressure found in the next level, *Condition Orange*. You know who's in front of you, to your sides and behind you. You don't think anyone will attack, but you are mentally prepared to react in the event of a conflict or confrontation. It is this level or condition where you should generally remain while engaged in your daily activities, as you are not placed under any significantly increased level of stress, but you are aware and therefore prepared to transition to *Condition Orange*, or higher, if the need arises.

Condition Orange

With *Condition Orange* you are keenly aware and may already sense that something is not right within your immediate environment. You may even feel that you might be attacked. Perhaps there are a number of suspicious men standing around your car, or perhaps you notice somebody is following you. You begin to assess the situation and seek out avenues of retreat and/or objects that will afford you cover or concealment should an attack occur or appear imminent.

Condition Red

You are under attack. Someone is assaulting you, and you are reacting to the attack and defending yourself. You are taking immediate and decisive action to stop your opponent by either engaging him or retreating to safety.

Summary

As we have seen from the list above, each level of awareness and the defensive countermeasures required, are built upon the previous in an escalating fashion. Now let's explore how we can apply the system in a hypothetical scenario. We can quickly dismiss *Condition White*, because being totally unprepared for any type of conflict or attack is an unacceptable state…unless you are asleep in your own bed.

Color Code Awareness Scenario

You leave the safety of your home or office to run a few

errands. It's a bright, clear day, and you are deeply focused on the task at hand. As you walk down the street, deep in thought, you are focused on just about everything except what's going on around you. Unbeknownst to you, a predator is watching you. The predator, a mugger, advances in your direction and before you are aware of him, he is directly in front of you, wielding a knife. He demands your money, and you comply because that is what you are told you should do by the police and major media. After he takes your money, he kills you. How did this happen? It happened because you were not paying attention. If you had been, you would have been aware of him long before he approached you and you would likely have been able to either retreat or respond in some other way, thus avoiding both the robbery and your death. While this may sound harsh, and is by no means intended to remove the responsibility from the attacker, *your death is as much your fault as it is your attacker's.*

Had you been aware of your surroundings, prepared for a possible attack and trained in proper countermeasures, the outcome would almost surely have been different.

Color Code Your Situational Awareness Level

If you're truly concerned about personal safety, your general state of alertness should always be *Condition Yellow*. This should be your minimum daily level and is appropriate for most situations. It is not possible, or necessary, to remain at a heightened state of alertness at all times (i.e., *Condition Orange*). When you go about your daily activities in a calm, relaxed and confident fashion, you are far less likely to become stressed out or exhaust your energies based upon perceived threats, which will inevitably lead to apathy should no attack occur. You will, however, be able to respond to events around you and avoid most trouble. Furthermore, under *Condition Yellow* you will be able to adjust to events and automatically shift into *Condition Orange* when needed.

But do not forget that maintaining a *Condition Orange* level of combat readiness for extended periods of time will drain you mentally and emotionally; you simply can't keep up that level of intensity for extended periods of time without adverse effects occurring. Don't even try. If you do, your capacity to remain alert will actually degrade. You could and likely will succumb to secondary psychological problems, such as paranoia, which will have you believing a terrorist or mugger is hiding behind every corner, intent on causing you harm.

The other possibility is apathy or burn out, which will impair your concentration and ability to think and function effectively during an actual hostile confrontation. Reserve *Condition Orange* for those times when a situation feels wrong, or your instincts tell you that there is danger about, but you cannot immediately identify the source. While in *Condition Orange*, you will be acutely aware of your surroundings and those people within them.

You should prepare for a conflict and even develop a plan of action prior to an event occurring within your immediate surrounding area.

Condition Red is not really an awareness level, since an attack is either imminent or already fully engaged. You have no choice but to stand and fight. While in *Condition Red*, violent and aggressive countermeasures are necessary, so you must remember that your only objective is to *win* the confrontation. Simply surviving is *not* an option, for as I have stated previously, simply surviving could imply several things, not the least of which is permanent injury.

Let's rerun the scenario described under *Condition White* with some important adjustments: You leave the safety of you home or office to run a few errands, and while you are walking down the sidewalk you notice several people standing around just ahead. One individual (about 50 yards away) stands out from the rest although he poses no immediate threat. He's not advancing in your direction or even looking at you, but there is something about him that makes you uneasy. The key is that under *Condition Yellow* you *notice* him. To be safe, you decide to cross the street and proceed on your way uninterrupted. By maintaining a preparedness state of *Condition Yellow* you have identified a potential threat and avoided a confrontation, by simply removing yourself from the environment.

Suddenly, the individual you observed crosses to your side of the street. Being instinctively alert, you realize circumstances have changed. You may be in trouble. Your level of alertness increases and you automatically adjust your alertness level to *Condition Orange*. The man is walking faster and closing the gap between you. Are you about to be attacked? It's a possibility and you start to formulate a countermeasure to whatever form the attack might take. You look around your immediate area for cover; you assess the chances of retreat, but heavy traffic may preclude you from crossing back across the street safely. If you are armed, you may prepare to draw your weapon and defend yourself. The individual begins to advance toward you more aggressively and appears to mimic your movements and begins to vocalize something that you cannot quite make out, but the tone of voce is aggressive in nature, his eyes appear wide and you notice that one of his hands is behind his back. This is *Condition Red*.

THE COMBAT MINDSET

Throughout the preceding section I have emphasized the concept of the need to *win* the conflict as opposed to simply surviving it. However we have not yet discussed what is required to do so. Now we will move on to perhaps the most critical element in winning a confrontation. Interestingly, the element is not entirely physical in nature, but it does rely on the most dangerous and powerful weapon we have available to us: our minds.

In order to win a confrontation there are several things to consider, including behaviors which must be taken into account and sometimes adjusted. In short, you must develop what is known as the *combat mindset*. In this section, we will be discussing these behaviors and the associated mental conditioning. It is, however, important to understand that a combat mindset includes more than just combat preparation. A combat mindset also includes pre-emptive or preventive measures.

Many think that people who take professional firearms training for self-defense are taught how to kill their opponent. This is simply not true. The truth is, the instinct to kill cannot be taught. It is a response triggered by a violent situation, and none of us can know how we will react until we face such an event. We can, however, develop what is known as a combat mindset, a mix of physical training and mental preparation which will greatly increase our ability to react accordingly or protect ourselves as well as friends and family. First, we will examine the *fight or flight* response that controls our behavior and how developing a combat mindset will train us to make the best defensive choice, automatically, without the need for further thought.

At this point, you are likely asking, what does any of this have to do with being situationally aware, avoiding a conflict, or dealing with a confrontation? Well, the answer is that by being prepared for an emergency *prior* to a situation developing, we will be one step ahead.

Just as we must be properly trained in weapons and tactics for personal defense, the combat mindset is something we all hope we will never need; however, developing the combat mindset *before* we need it means that there is one less thing to think about when the unthinkable occurs. Should it occur anyway, those who are better prepared, both mentally and physically are those who will generally win.

Fight or flight response

Some people are convinced that if attacked, they would not hesitate to engage their attacker. Others will tell you they couldn't possibly take a life. But until you've been in that situation, it is virtually impossible to predict your own behavior. This is because what really controls our actions in a violent confrontation is the *fight or flight* response, which is a primitive, automatic and innate fundamental psychological response to any perceived threat to our survival.

Once activated, this response results in a series of physiological changes involving the release of specialized chemicals and hormones including adrenaline, noradrenaline, and cortisol into the bloodstream. The respiratory rate increases; blood moves from the digestive tract to the muscles of the body; pupils dilate to allow for greater amounts of light; and increased perception and our impulses are more rapidly acted upon. In addition, our perception of pain is minimized. In short, we achieve a heightened awareness of our surroundings coupled with a strong instinct to either flee from the confrontation or stand and fight.

Unfortunately, sometimes this condition creates a state of mind in which the perception of danger reaches a level of paranoia, wherein we perceive danger from virtually every side, even where none exists. This is where training comes in. While it is not possible to train someone to control the actual response of *fight or flight*, with the proper training we *can* learn to control what we do with it. It is an accepted principle that when a person is trained to handle any situation, he generally reverts to the training he received when a similar situation actually occurs. This is also the case when the situation involves a violent confrontation.

Here's an example of the *fight or flight* mechanism in action. Imagine it's 2:00 am, and you are walking home from a night out with friends. You see a group of teenagers ahead who appear to be up to no good. You come to this conclusion based on both the activities they are engaged in and by the fact that you begin to feel anxious or a chill runs down your spine. You decide to cross the street and take an alternate route home. You arrive home safely and all is well. In this case, your flight reaction helped you avoid the potential danger. But you could just as easily have responded with the instinct to fight and decided to continue on your current path, proceed through the group, and perhaps still arrived home without incident. On the other hand, your decision to move closer to the group may have antagonized one of the group members and resulted in a conflict.

When the terrorists overtook Flight 93 on 11 September 2001, several passengers rose up and attempted counter the actions of the terrorists who were in control of the plane. While I was not aboard this flight, I believe I can safely say that some of the passengers were either unable or unwilling to become involved in any effort to defend themselves or the plane. This behavior was directly related to their *fight or flight* response and their minds caused them to escape the conflict by effectively shutting down and accepting their fate. Others, however, where motivated to a sense of aggression, in spite of the fear they were feeling. They developed a plan and executed it. Although the effort was not successful, the act itself demonstrates courage, which is the ability to function in the face of fear.

Sometimes just one aspect of a situation will trigger our response. Take the case of a mother and child. They are exiting a store when an armed attacker attempts to take the child. Instinctively, *most* mothers will ignore almost any personal risk in order to protect their child. However, the same woman, attacked when she is alone, probably would attempt to escape (flight) if possible and only resist (fight) if escape seemed impossible.

Combat mindset provides a fighting chance

None of us can predict how we will react in a violent confrontation unless we have been exposed to similar events in the past. But by developing a combat mindset, the chances of taking the best action possible will be significantly increased. Again, training will not override the *fight or flight* response, but learning the right techniques, tactics and weapon craft will provide you with a good base of counteractions to choose from. In addition, chances are that you *will* fall back on your training, when faced with a situation that warrants violent force.

It's similar to defensive driving. Say you're in light traffic and something distracts your attention for a moment. You turn back to discover that the car just ahead has stopped and you're closing in rapidly. Instinctively, you apply the brake and turn the steering wheel hard to one side. This response, which successfully avoids a collision with the other vehicle, is automatic. Had you taken time to think, you probably would have collided. The same principle applies to personal defense and is equally valid, whether used with a firearm, a club, knife or any other weapon.

To increase your chance of success, your body and mind must be in synch. The physical aspects of performing the necessary tactics and techniques are relatively easy to learn. When learning to use a handgun for self-defense, for example, the emphasis is on the mechanics of gun handling, loading, safety, accuracy, drawing from a holster and using cover and concealment. But in addition, all my students also learn situational awareness and the importance of conflict avoidance.

Physical preparation is only half of the combat craft. We need mental preparation to give us confidence in our abilities and to affirm our right to defend our lives and the lives of those around us. The mental aspect is harder to instill, in large part due to training that began in early childhood. Growing up, most of us were instructed not to fight, to strive to be good and avoid violence. While these are all good beliefs, our own defense must always come first, for if we are injured or dead, we cannot protect those around us. The combat mindset requires us to recognize that there are times when the *only* way to survive a situation is to fight and fight to *win*.

Part of your mental preparedness is your willingness to justify deadly force. In order to reach a point where you are confident in the choice to harm or even kill another in self-defense, it is important to have an understanding of the role of the police in society. First, you need to understand that the police do not have any obligation to protect an *individual*; rather, their job is to protect *society*, as a whole. This surprises most people. But a quick review of case law shows that a surprising number of cases brought by individuals against the police for failure to protect them, even after repeated calls for help, are simply dismissed. Here are just a few such cases.

In Warren *v.* District of Columbia, the court expressed itself succinctly: it is the "fundamental principle of American law that a government and its agents are under no general duty to provide public services, such as police protection, to any individual citizen." In Hartzler v. City of San Jose, 46 Cal. App. 3d 6 (1st Dist. 1975) the court held that the San Jose police were not liable for ignoring Mrs. Brunell's pleas for help. And in Riss v. New York, 240 N.E.2d 860 (N.Y. 1968) where a young women was attacked and permanently disfigured from the effects of lye (which was thrown in her face by her ex-boyfriend, who had been stalking her) the City of New York prevented her from arming herself and then denied all responsibility to provide her with protection, *even after multiple requests had been made.*

Another case worthy of note is DeShaney v. Winnebago County Department of Social Services (109 S. Ct. 998, 1989). In this case, DeShaney (the injured party) was a boy who had been beaten and permanently injured by his father. He claimed a "special relationship" existed because local officials knew he was being abused, but the court held that no duty arose because of a "special relationship," and concluded that Constitutional duties of care and protection only exist with regard to certain individuals, such as incarcerated prisoners, involuntarily committed mental patients and others restrained against their will, *which would make them incapable of protecting themselves.*

The preceding examples of actual case law demonstrate that, contrary to popular belief, the police do not have a duty or obligation to protect individual citizens. They are presented so that you, the reader, can better understand the importance of learning methods of self-protection and defense; because ultimately, the responsibility for your personal safety belongs to *you.*

What's more, we cannot expect other people to come to our defense. We live in a litigious society. We're all afraid of being sued--by our attackers (which is outrageous)--or by bystanders who might be hurt accidentally. This has left far too many people concerned about personal liability should they defend themselves, let alone intervene in the defense of anyone else. If you doubt me, consider a conversation I had with an acquaintance, who is also a proponent of personal defense and firearm ownership. I began by asking him to consider the following scenario:

You are on your way home from work. It is dark. You are legally armed with a pistol, which is properly concealed. As you exit the building, you hear a woman screaming, "Help, he is going to kill me!" As you look over to the source of the disturbance, you see a six-foot, 240-pound male dragging the screaming woman, who appears to weigh perhaps 120 pounds, off to a darkened area of the parking lot. My question was, "Do you get involved?" The answer he provided, I must admit, surprised me. He said, "No, I would not get involved." When I asked why not, he said that it was not for fear for his life, rather for fear of losing his permit to carry a weapon, then being sued and potentially losing his house. So I changed the scenario. I told him that the woman being dragged off was his daughter. I asked if he would expect someone else to intervene. His answer was quick and resounding: "Yes."

I would have been less surprised if his reason for not wishing to become involved in the first scenario were based primarily on fear for his own personal safety. I would have accepted that, albeit grudgingly. However, he was clearly more concerned about losing personal property and suffering the legal repercussions of the intervention than he was in fear for his life. It is also worth noting that at no time did I suggest that he had to use a weapon to help, I merely asked if he would become involved. He could have simply contacted the police, yelled for the attacker to stop, or sounded his car's horn to draw attention to the area. Instead, he chose to do *nothing*.

If my friend's attitude is indicative of society's overall attitude, which statistics would appear to support, then while we do expect others to help us, we are not prepared to do the same for them. And while I am not advocating vigilantism or any other behavior that would suggest one should use force against another without justification, I do believe that we cannot expect to receive assistance from others if we are not prepared to provide it ourselves.

One final note: If you do find yourself in a violent encounter and manage to secure the safety of your family, and you, yourself, are no longer in danger, you *must* resist the temptation to return to your attacker and continue your assault. While you do have the right to defend yourself, you do not have the right to use excessive or unreasonable force.

If you do that, then you will be no better than your attacker. In addition, your plan to seek vengeance may backfire. There is an old saying: *"He who seeks vengeance should first dig two graves."*

Throughout this section we have focused mostly on concepts of combat and the basic mental preparations that will assist you in making a decision on whether to choose fight or flight. What we have not discussed are the components of the combat mindset that are necessary to *win* a confrontation. And as I've said before, it is not enough to survive a violent confrontation--you must *win* it.

Tips for winning a violent confrontation

In order to win in a violent conflict, it is critical that the following principles be observed; for failure to do so can, and often will, lead to injury or even death.

☐ *Your opponent is at least as skilled as you are.* By taking this position, you will not become overly confident and will be less likely to make a mistake which could cost you your life.

☐ *Do not loose your self-control and allow yourself to make foolish mistakes.* You must focus on the task at hand as if your life depends upon it, because it does. As in any confrontation, whether it is physical or verbal, the moment composure is lost, the battle is lost. In the words of Sun Tzu: *"The General, unable to control his irritation, will launch his men to the assault like swarming ants, with the result of one third being slain, while the town still remains untaken."* Your goal is to remain calm and focused so that if anybody loses self-control, it will be your opponent, which can lead to a mistake which you can use to your advantage.

☐ *Continually seek an avenue of retreat.* It is not your responsibility to engage an attacker beyond the point of your security or safety (or that of another). The moment you have the opportunity to retreat to safety you must attempt to do so. This is important in terms of your legal liability but also because the longer the confrontation continues, the more likely you will be to make a serious, and perhaps even fatal, mistake.

☐ ***Never trap or "box in" your attacker.*** After all, who is the most dangerous man in the world? The man who has nothing to lose. Like an animal, if cornered, your attacker may actually become more aggressive.

☐ ***Try to think like your opponent.*** There is an old saying: *"Those who hunt monsters must take great care that they do not become as monsters themselves."* This saying likely came about because in order to track and capture a criminal, it is first necessary to understand the criminal mind. This is why security consultants are often asked to read security protocols. They are hired to identify flaws and to recommend counter measures should security be breached. They know the mind of the criminal element-- so they know what to protect against. So, while you can't be expected to know the specific personality of your attacker, you can attempt to use what you do know. For example, are they on drugs? Are they out for money? Are they gang-bangers trying to impress other gang members? Pick up as much as you can, using your training in situational awareness, and it will serve you well; for the more you know about your opponent, the more likely you will be effectively anticipate and counter their actions.

☐ ***Whenever possible, cheat!*** Remember that what we are discussing here is not a school yard fist fight, but a fight for your life. If a violent conflict cannot be avoided, seek out and exploit *every* weaknesses in your attacker, as there is no such thing as a "fair" fight. This is another example where situational awareness comes into play. Lets say that you are walking down the street and you observe an individual acting suspiciously. As he advances toward you, your alertness level increases. You observe that he is limping, and is favoring his right leg. Is he faking it? Perhaps, but you really don't know. He attempts to accost you, and you are required to defend yourself. What should be your primary target for any countermeasures not involving a weapon? The correct and obvious answer is his right leg. Why? Well, because he appears to be favoring this limb, and if it is truly injured, it will present a weak point, which should be exploited to its fullest advantage.

☐ ***Deceit and subterfuge are your allies when engaged in a violent confrontation.*** Once again we can refer to a principle found within the works of Sun Tzu and the *Art of War,* which reads: *"Hold out baits and fain disorder and crush him."* This tactic can actually be quite effective. I personally have used it with success in the past. It's a simple tactic, which will become clear from the following story. An associate and I were preparing to engage within "Force on Force" training using paintball guns. For some reason, my associate started firing rapidly in my direction prior to the official start of our exercise. I immediately yelled for him to stop, and was repeatedly ignored. I was struck twice in the leg with a paintball at a distance of approximately 7 - 10 feet. Now it is important to understand, that the average paintball is moving at a speed of between 200 - 300 FPS (feet per second), and they do hurt on impact. So I decided to teach this individual a lesson I am sure he will never forget. I immediately feigned an injury by grabbing my leg and began yelling. Then I began to limp in his direction while playing on his sympathies. As a result, he made a fatal mistake: he let down his guard. As soon as I was within a close enough range to effectively make my point, I lifted my head, looked him straight in the eyes, and "Yea, I'm fine" as I fired a single paintball directly at his thigh. The look on his face was priceless, and was matched only by his physical reaction to being hit at such a close range.

While I do not recommend that you try this, it does offer a prime example of how to use deceit and subterfuge to obtain an edge over an opponent or attacker. (I should also state, that neither of us suffered any permanent damage, as we were both wearing protective clothing designed for this purpose).

To end this section, here is another relevant quote from Sun Tuz's *The Art of War:*

"If you know the enemy and know yourself, you need not fear the result of a hundred battles. If you know yourself but not your enemy, for every victory gained you will also suffer a defeat. If you know neither the enemy nor yourself, you will succumb in every battle."

The essential principles of victory

Throughout this text I have provided references to the works of Sun Tzu. While the quotes I have cited were originally designed for military combat applications, I believe they are equally relevant to civilian combat scenarios. The list below is a modified version of Sun Tzu's *Five Essential Principles of Victory* and is useful in understanding the components of success in battle.

He shall win who knows when to fight and when not to. This is closely related to the concept of situational awareness. Awareness of your surroundings and potential confrontations will allow you to more accurately assess your chances of success in a conflict as well as your ability to retreat to safety.

He shall win who understands how to deal with both superior as well as inferior opponents. Having the skill to dominate and/or destroy your opponent does not mean you should automatically use it. For example: If you are attacked by an old woman with a cane and she is clearly not a threat to you, should you use overwhelming force to incapacitate her? No. The correct action under these circumstances would be to simply retreat. In this scenario, the old woman is an example of an *inferior* opponent. Conversely, if your attacker is significantly younger than you and is in better physical condition, say buffed and 30 pounds lighter than you, and retreat is *not* a viable option, you had better engage this *superior* force with as much violence, speed and aggression as possible in order to terminate the confrontation as quickly as possible. Remember, protracted combat against a superior opponent never ends well.

He shall win whose army is animated by the same spirit throughout all its ranks. While this principle may appear on its face to be directed at a number of persons engaged in a conflict, the core of the statement is found in the term "spirit," which is to say that there must be uniform desire to be victorious. In other words, if your heart is not in it, you will lose the battle and possibly, even your life.

He shall win who, prepared himself, waits to take the enemy unprepared. Again, we return to an aspect of situational awareness and the combat mindset. As I have stated earlier, being situationally aware of your environment and potential threats will often provide you with the opportunity to watch for and exploit weaknesses or behaviors which your attacker will not anticipate.

Physical components to winning a violent conflict

First, remember that once an attack is fully engaged you must immediately switch to an offensive posture and present a counter-attack with as much speed, surprise and violence of action as possible, while maintaining self control. Consider the motto of the United States DELTA Force, considered to be the best of the best in the world of anti-terrorism. Their insignia reads: *"Speed, Surprise, and Violence of Action."* Below we will discuss each of these elements and how they should be applied in a violent confrontation.

☐ *Speed*—Once a violent confrontation begins, there is

little time to think about what is happening. Your reactions must be dynamic and automatic. This is where the element of speed comes in. Once attacked, you must immediately switch from a defensive posture to an offensive posture. As Sun Tzu states *"Security against defeat implies defensive tactics; ability to defeat the enemy means taking the offensive."*

☐ **Surprise**—The second element necessary to win a violent confrontation is surprise. When you take the offensive even as you are being attacked, you have an automatic advantage, in that your attacker will not expect it; for it is accepted as fact that your attacker perceived you as weak when you were selected as a victim. Again, in the words of Sun Tzu: *"Standing on the defensive indicates insufficient strength; while attacking, a superabundance of strength."* This superabundance of strength will almost always surprise your attacker, so use it to your advantage.

☐ **Violence**—The third and final element necessary to win a violent confrontation is the willingness to use rapid and violently aggressive force against your attacker.

In the words of Sun Tzu: *"Hence the skillful fighter puts himself into a position which makes defeat impossible, and does not miss the moment for defeating the enemy."*

Basic Combat Shooting Fundamentals

The basic fundamentals of shooting are contained in a set of guidelines that will be the focus of this chapter. While the basics of target and defensive shooting are similar, when you shift from target to defensive shooting, there are a number of additional factors to consider.

We'll begin this section with basic shooting fundamentals which include the following:

- ☐ The aspects of the human body
- ☐ Firearm safety rules
- ☐ Handgun and holster selection
- ☐ Basic combat shooting fundamentals
- ☐ Proper shot placement
- ☐ Self-diagnosis and correction of common shooting errors.

Identifying aspects of the human body

As we mentioned in an earlier section of this book, if a shooter is right-handed then the right side of his body is considered his *master* side and the left side of his body is considered his *support* side. The same distinction holds true when referring to legs, hands, feet, etc. However, when discussing the eyes we do not use the terms master and support, rather we use the terms *dominant* and *non-dominant.*

It is possible, and not uncommon, for an individual to be right side *master* and left eye *dominant.* In some cases, as well, the reverse is true. Neither of these present a significant problem for the shooter, but may require the shooter to receive a some additional training in order to become proficient in shooting techniques.

The following image depicts the aspects of the human body as it is divided into both the master and support sides, within an individual who is right handed and facing you.

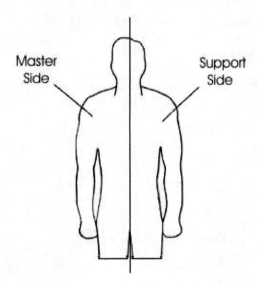

Firearm safety

The rules of safe gun handling should become second nature if you practice them regularly. The following safety rules represent the *Critical 4* and other rules of firearm safety and they should all be applied at all times as applicable. As stated earlier, by ingraining these behaviors in yourself, you will not need to think about how to handle your firearm when a conflict erupts or other activities require it.

The Critical 4:

1. ***Treat every weapon as if it were loaded.*** A simple phrase to remember is "Action open equals weapon safe; action closed equals weapon live." It is extremely important to remember this. *When the action of a weapon is open, it cannot fire.*

2. *Never point at anything you don't intend to shoot.* And never point the weapon in a direction in which an accidental discharge will cause harm. The only safe direction is the one which will not do damage to anyone or anything should the weapon be discharged. In a house, the safest direction is angled toward the floor with the muzzle of the weapon pointing to a corner where the supporting joints of the structure meet. To help us with this idea, we rely on the *laser rule.* While primarily used for dynamic (tactical) entries, the laser rule is a safety technique in which an imaginary laser line is drawn from the muzzle of the weapon outward until it makes contact with the nearest object. This line should never cross anything which is not an accepted target. This principle should be applied every time the weapon is removed from its holster. During a dynamic entry, each member of a team will be responsible for a specific area. This is pre-planned to reduce the chance of the laser rule being violated against another team member. This same principle should be applied anytime an individual is carrying a firearm for any purpose.

3. *Keep your finger off the trigger until you intend to shoot.* There is a natural tendency for people who are new to firearms to place their finger inside the trigger guard. This must be avoided in order to prevent an accidental discharge. Any time you are not engaging a hostile target, even if you are scanning or searching for an attacker, the trigger finger should be resting along the frame of the weapon and should only be moved inside the trigger guard once the target has been identified and the decision to engage has been made.

4. *Always know your target, backstop and have a reasonable idea of what is beyond.* As important as it is to know your target, it is equally important to know what is behind your target and, if possible, beyond. Remember: a bullet will travel a considerable distance and the shooter is responsible for everything the bullet comes in contact with once the weapon is fired.

Other Safety Rules:

As important as the rules listed above, are the following safety rules which will apply to other activities involving the use and storage of firearms.

1. *Always be sure the firearm is safe to operate.* Before you begin to fire the firearm, inspect it for any signs of excessive wear (i.e. cracks in the frame, obstructions in the bore, etc.). If anything suspicious is found, *DO NOT* fire the weapon until it has been check by a competent person.

2. *Know how to safely operate the firearm.* While there are only two traditional types of handguns (Revolvers & Semi-Automatics), there are several different model, some of which will function differently based upon the specific manufacturer. Before you attempt to operate a firearm with which you are not familiar, first either read the manual or consult a competent person or instructor.

3. *Always use the correct ammunition for the firearm.* Ammunition sizing is identified by caliber. The term caliber is a measurement used to identify the distance between the lands or interior surface of the bore which measured in millimeters or hundredths of an inch (i.e. 9mm = .355 hundredths of an inch). Most firearms are caliber specific, however in some cases a cartridge of a similar size can be forced into a chamber and discharged. The problem with this is the pressures involved in the discharge can damage the firearm and cause personal injury.

4. *Always use eye and ear protection when appropriate.* It need not be said that the report (bang) heard when a firearm is discharged is loud. However extensive exposure to this level of noise can and often will cause hearing loss. Therefore whenever possible, hearing protection should be used. In addition to the report of a discharged firearm, there is also the consideration of the gases and debris which are released during this action. These gases and debris are extremely heated and will cause injury if they

come in contact with the eye. Therefore, as with hearing protection, whenever appropriate (i.e. on the range) proper eye protection should be used at all times.

5. *Never use alcohol or drugs while carrying or shooting a firearm.* In addition to this action being illegal and foolish, the introduction of narcotic drugs or alcohol into the bloodstream will often impair an individuals ability to use reason and exercise proper judgment.

6. *All firearms should always be stored is such a manner as to assist in the prevention of unauthorized persons gaining access to them.* In most jurisdictions, the practice of storing firearms in a secure manner to prevent unauthorized persons from gaining access to them is a law. However even in jurisdictions where this is not the case, it is a reasonable and correct practice to adhere to.

7. *Never carry or use a firearm while in a state of extreme anger or depression.* As with the introduction of drugs or alcohol into the blood stream, when an individual is under extreme effects of anger or depression, the ability to reason or exercise proper judgment will often be compromised.

8. *All owners of firearms are responsible for the instructing of their children in the actions they should take if they encounter an unattended firearm.* Children will generally have a natural curiosity toward firearms. One method of instructing children is as follows:

1. When the child *FIRST* expresses *ANY* interest or curiosity towards firearms, sit down with them and an *UNLOADED* firearm. Allow them to handle the gun and ask questions. Explain that it is *NOT* a toy, and that they should never handle a gun without an adult present. The reason to *NEVER* simply say *DON'T TOUCH*, is that this will often increase the curiosity level and can lead to the child seeking out a firearm.

2. The next thing to instruct the child in is the behavior to take should they ever encounter an unattended firearm.

- ☐ Stop
- ☐ Don't Touch
- ☐ Leave The Area
- ☐ Find And Tell An Adult

Grip

Grip is one of the first components of shooting fundamentals. While there are several different techniques that may be used in gripping your weapon, I will only be covering two of them here. One works quite well, the other, not so well.

Cup & Saucer: This technique is performed by gripping the pistol with the master hand and placing the palm of the support hand underneath the master hand while resting it against the butt of the gun or magazine well. The main problem with this gripping technique is the lack of support it provides to the master hand and the potential of the support hand to pull the muzzle of the pistol downward, causing your shots to hit low on the target. I do not recommend this technique.

The illustration, below, demonstrates the Cup & Saucer

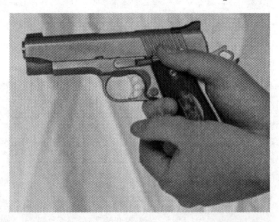

The High Thumb Carry: An alternate to the technique, above, is the high thumb carry. This technique may feel strange at first, but most find that after giving it some time to become comfortable, it provides an increased ability to control the weapon and recoil, thus increasing the ability to shoot more accurately and more quickly.

The High Thumb Carry is performed as follows: Begin by firmly, but not overly tightly, gripping the pistol with the master hand, insuring that the webbing between the thumb and pointer finger is placed as high as possible and comfortably into the backstrap of the weapon which is located between the grip panels. Then place the heel of the support hand against the exposed area of the grip panel, filling the open space with the support side fingers wrapped around the front and on top of the master hand fingers, which are underneath the trigger guard. Some shooters prefer to place the index finger of the support hand in front of the trigger guard. This variation does not necessarily present a problem; however, some do tend to fire low on their targets when using this variation of the *high thumb carry* technique.

The illustration, below, demonstrates the High Thumb Carry

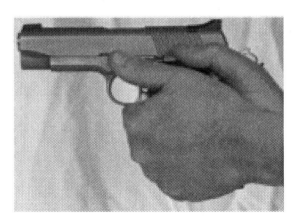

As stated above, the primary benefit to this gripping technique is found in the ability to better control the weapon and subsequent recoil, as a greater degree of the frame is covered by both hands, which will help to reduce the amount of reset time required between shots because of the increased recoil control.

Stance

The next principle we will discuss is the stance. Whether you are target shooting or combat shooting, the key to a proper stance is balance. Proper balance when shooting is directly related to accuracy for a number of reasons. One of the most important reasons, is your ability to minimize body movement, also called the *arc* of movement.

In the realm of combat and defensive tactical shooting, there are very few absolutes. However, among them is the ultra-importance of a correct and effective shooting stance. There are two main types of shooting stance, the *Weaver* and the *Isosceles*. There are also countless variations thereof and neither is inherently better than the other, provided the basic required principles are observed. In this section, I will explain the core components of both of these of shooting stances, as well as how they are utilized.

Balance:

The most important component of a combat shooting stance is balance. Why? Well if you are not balanced, with both feet flat on the ground, the potential for unwanted movement will be increased. Any movement, regardless of how slight, will be dramatically reflected in the degradation of your accuracy. So how does one achieve this balance?

To begin with we need to go back to the basic principles of combat marksmanship, which include the aspects of the body: *master* side and the *support* side. As stated earlier, the master side of the body is determined by the hands of the shooter. Whichever hand maintains the primary control of the weapon, will be considered the master side of the body, and this will be reflected as well with the legs and feet. In order to have proper balance, both feet *must* be flat on the ground, and should be placed shoulder-width apart. The support side foot should be forward of the master side foot, with the toes of the master foot in line with the arch of the support foot.

Next the knees should be slightly bent to allow for the mass of the body weight to be placed upon the lower extremities, and the body proper should lean forward, slightly, to assist in the control of recoil by placing body weight and mass behind the weapon. With this position, rapid movement is made possible, as your body is already in a posture of movement. But remember that this is only a guideline, and should be used as such. There is no hard and fast rule which does not allow for variation *provided balance is achieved.*

Head position:

Another principle of a proper stance is the correct placement of the shooter's head and chin. A common problem with handgun shooters is shooting too low or too high on the target. This is often caused by the position of the shooter's head. The reason for this is that a handgun, which is a weighted object, will cause the arms to be pushed downward by the force of gravity. At the same time, the shooter's chin will instinctively tilt forward to allow for the sights to be aligned. Stated another way, the weapon is in control of the shooter and not the other way around. This will cause the shots to hit low on the target. In some cases, the shooter may attempt to overcompensate and the chin will be tilted too far back. This will cause the shots to hit high on the target. The correct method of chin placement is to maintain the head and chin level and to bring the sights of the weapon up to the level of the shooter's eyes.

This is not as easy as it sounds and will require extensive practice. If you have trouble with this you may purchase a cervical collar from a surgical supply store. This device will force your head and chin to remain level and will assist with the development of the muscle memory over time.

Movement:

Any combat stance or position must allow the shooter the ability of free movement. This means that the shooter must be able to rapidly and aggressively respond to any situation which arises both when the weapon is drawn from its holster as well as when it is still secured. For example, when shooting from behind a cover point, you need to be sure that you are far enough away from the wall of the cover position to allow for a full range of view and motion, while not compromising your position or over exposing yourself to your opponent.

This is accomplished by proper positioning of the feet and will change depending on the side you are using cover from. If you are engaging a target from your master side, your master foot will be forward of your support foot and the support foot will rotate out on the ball of the foot, allowing for target to be acquired and the sights to be aligned.

If you are not using cover, but are simply having a conversation, you still need to be aware of your feet in order to move quickly if the situation should require it. In this case, your master side, which is the side where your weapon is kept, should be angled or bladed away from the person you are conversing with and your support side foot should be pointing forward, toward the person with whom you are speaking. You should keep both hands centered over your torso, vertically, although they may be positioned horizontally either high or low.

Your hands should *never* be placed in your pockets. And any items, such as keys, pocket watches, etc., should be held with the support hand only. This is to ensure that you have the ability to protect the weapon should someone attempt to take it from your holster.

Recoil control:

There is a myth which says that the recoil (or kick as it is commonly called) of some handguns can knock the shooter to the ground. This is not true. However, recoil from a handgun *can* be a major contributor to the placement of inaccurate shots.

This is why the proper shooting stance includes position the feet shoulder-width apart and flat on the ground, with knees bent, body mass forward, and the wrists elbows and shoulders in their proper position (locked straight out for the *Isosceles* and correctly bent for the *Weaver*). By maintaining the correct body position, the energy released by the recoil will be countered by the mass of the body, as opposed to only the arms. In addition, as the released energy applies force against an object of increased mass (i.e. the body of the shooter) the reverse mass will force the weapon to return forward after the shot is fired. This allows the shooter to regain faster control, and reacquisition of the sights, for follow up shots to be fired.

As stated earlier, the two most common shooting stances are the *Isosceles* and the *Weaver*. The *Isosceles* is inherently more stable than the *Weaver*, however, thanks to Hollywood, most people insist on using the *Weaver* stance. While there is nothing wrong with the *Weaver* stance, it can be difficult, and in some cases uncomfortable, to perform correctly. Therefore, when most shooters attempt to use the *Weaver*, they are actually performing a modified *Weaver*. When this happens, they are often relying on their arms, alone, to resist the recoil of the weapon and, as discussed, above, this may impact their ability to regain control, reacquisition the sights and continue shooting.

Now let's take a look at how to perform the above referenced stances. We'll begin with the *Isosceles* stance.

The Isosceles stance:

☐ Place both feet flat on the ground, shoulder-width apart.

☐ Knees should be slightly bent, with the majority of your body weight placed on your lower extremities.

- [ ] For a target shooting stance, the toes of both feet should be in alignment with each other. For a combat or defense stance, the master foot should be in alignment with the arch of the support foot.

- [ ] Both master and support wrists and elbows should be locked out straight in front of you and your head and chin should be level so that you are looking straight ahead. Your body should be directly facing and in line with the target.

The above illustration demonstrates the Isosceles stance

The Weaver Stance:

- [ ] As with the Isosceles stance, begin by placing both feet flat on the ground, shoulder-width apart.

- [ ] Your master side arm should be locked straight out in front of you as you apply a pushing motion to the weapon with the master hand. Meanwhile, the support side hand should be bent at the elbow and should provide a pulling motion so as to lock the weapon in place.

☐ Rotate the shoulder and elbow of your support side arm inward toward the center of your chest. This will cause your body to blade, making it appear perpendicular to the target, which is actually beneficial as it will provide for a smaller target area being presented to your attacker.

With both of these stances it is important to lean into the weapon (although the lean is less prominent with the *Weaver* stance) allowing your body mass to be behind the shot. This will allow the body to absorb the recoil of the weapon. It will also allow for a significant decrease in what is known as *reset time*. This is the amount of time necessary to reacquire your sights after each shot is fired. The overall objective is to have as short a reset time as possible between shots.

The illustration, below, demonstrates the Weaver stance

Trigger control

The term trigger control is used to describe the proper method of activating the trigger on a firearm. A commonly used, but erroneous expression, found in Hollywood and often used by the media, is to "pull the trigger." In actuality, the trigger of a firearm should never be pulled, as this will cause the muzzle to move in a side-to-side motion, causing inaccurate shot placement. But before we discuss the proper way to activate a trigger, we need to discuss how to apply the trigger finger to the trigger.

Proper placement of your finger on the trigger is as follows: place the center of the pad of the index finger, between the tip and the first knuckle joint, directly against the trigger. Once the correct placement is achieved, the trigger must be squeezed or pressed, not pulled, in one smooth and continuous movement. This technique requires some practice, but once you are proficient in it you will see improved shooting results.

Breath control

There are three accepted techniques for breath control while shooting.

Technique 1—The first technique, commonly taught by the National Rifle Association (NRA) is performed as follows.

☐ Take a deep breath.

☐ Exhale approximately half of the breath.

☐ Hold your breath with air still in your lungs.

☐ Discharge your weapon.

While this technique will work fine for target shooting, it does have some inherent problems. Among the biggest is that if the breath is held too long, muscle tremors may occur. This is caused by a physiological condition known as *hypoxia*, which, in layman's terms, simply means that the muscles are oxygen deprived.

When such tremors occur, naturally, the shooter's accuracy will be diminished.

Technique 2—The second technique, and the one I prefer,

involves simply shooting between breaths, rather than attempting to shoot while holding the breath. With this technique, the muscle tremors are not usually a problem as there is no build up of pressure in the chest, and the average human being will breath an average of 12 – 20 breaths per minute, which allows for a significant amount of time to align the weapons sights and accurately discharge the weapon. Additionally, during a pause in your breathing your body can more easily be kept still, which aids in more accurate shooting.

However, both of the above techniques are virtually useless in a violent confrontation. This is because during a violent confrontation it is highly unlikely that you will have the presence of mind to focus on your breathing. Instead, all of your attention will be focused on the threat. In this situation, a third technique is preferred.

Technique 3—This technique is known as *scan and breathe*. It should be used immediately after the first series of shots are fired, while you are scanning for additional threats. The technique is performed, as follows:

☐ The weapon is returned to what is known as the *high ready position*, which we will discuss in greater detail later.

☐ While turning from side to side, at the waist, seeking additional threats, the shooter concentrates on inhaling and exhaling as naturally as possible.

Sight alignment

Proper Sight Alignment, one of the two most important shooting fundamentals, is really quite easy. But if not performed correctly, all of the other principles or fundamentals, no matter how well they are performed, will do little to assure shooting accuracy.

Proper alignment of the sights are performed by aligning the front sight (located just above the muzzle) with the rear sight, which is located just in front of the hammer, at the rear of the gun. The front sight should be viewed through the notch of the rear sight and be level across the top, with an equal distance on each side of the rear notch.

The following illustration demonstrates the proper placement of the front sight within the notch of the rear sight.

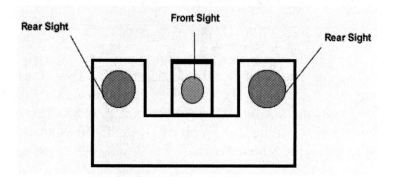

Once you have obtained proper sight alignment during target shooting, you will need to focus on something. That said, it is time for another basic human anatomy lesson. The human eye is only capable of focusing on one object at a time. Therefore when lining up your sights, what should you focus on? The target? No. The rear sight? No. The front sight? Yes. Your eye should focus on the *front* sight, and while you should still be able to see the target, it should appear out of focus or blurred.

This requirement however, is a bit different when it comes to combat shooting. During a violent confrontation, it is extremely important that you do not lose sight of your attacker. Therefore, the following sight alignment technique is recommended for use in such a situation.

☐ Keep your eye on your attacker.

☐ Draw the pistol from the holster while maintaining visual contact with the attacker.

☐ Focus on the attacker's center of mass (COM) while

allowing your peripheral vision to monitor his extremities for clues to his next move.

☐ Bring your weapon up to your eye allowing the front site of your weapon to *break* the line of sight between your eye and your attacker's body.

☐ Once the proper alignment has been achieved, exhale and before taking your next breath discharge your weapon.

Muscle memory

Although it is not, technically, a fundamental of shooting, the principle known as *muscle memory* cannot be overlooked when addressing principles of marksmanship. We've all heard the axiom "practice makes perfect." The truth is actually *"perfect* practice makes perfect." Unfortunately, no human being is perfect or is likely to ever be perfect. However, with the correct amount of training and effort our skills can be increased dramatically. So in this section I will provide you with techniques you can practice to develop *muscle memory.*

Human beings are creatures of habit. The simplest proof of it is that the more we perform a specific task, the better we become at its execution. However, it must be stated that proper initial training is essential to ensure correct technique. So lets begin by thinking back to when you were first learning to ride a bicycle. The first few times you mounted and began to pedal you were most likely nervous and felt off balance, but as time progressed, you began to feel more confident and soon your were riding along with almost no thought, right?

Well, the same holds true for shooting. The first time you fire a firearm of any type you are likely to be nervous, mainly because you do not know what to expect. But again, as time progresses and you continue to shoot, you will become more accustomed to the noise and recoil. This comfort level is actually a result of *muscle memory.*

Muscle memory is a pre-determined behavior that your mind

assigns to a specific action. For example, when properly instructed, a well-practiced defensive shooter should be able to draw a pistol from a holster and acquire the proper grip, sight alignment and stance, in one fluid motion without excessive/unnecessary movement. In addition, with continued practice, that same shooter will be able to reduce his presentation, set and reset times, thereby increasing his chances of prevailing in a violent confrontation.

In other words, we develop muscle memory by training and regular practice. For our purposes, we will consider "regular" to mean a minimum of 20 minutes per day at least three times per week. Now, this may sound difficult to do, particularly since some of the techniques will require the use of a shooting range and live ammunition, but not all. For instance, drawing, reloading and clearing stoppages can all be practiced in the comfort of your own home. Any instructor can also assist you in procuring training rounds, which are plastic cartridges specifically designed for the purpose outlined herein. In addition to the physical techniques described above, you can also develop imaginary scenarios and seek to take appropriate action. Again, this is something your instructor can assist you with.

All of these things will, over time, develop your muscle memory, which can also be thought of as *reactionary movement* as opposed to instinct, which is a principle which cannot be taught, as although instinct is the basic tool animals use to survive, and while most people do not like to admit it, human beings are in many ways nothing more than animals themselves. Therefore, we are all subject to the same primal behaviors. Which brings us to another area of contention: *point shooting*.

Point shooting is nothing more than the name implies; it is pointing in the direction of the target and shooting. While some might argue that this is *instinctive* shooting, I disagree, as stated above, an instinct cannot be taught. Additionally I do not generally recommend the practice of point shooting due to the high probability of misses. This is not to say that point shooting has no place, but within general confrontations it is my opinion that there is no place for point shooting. *Reactive* shooting, however, is based deeply in muscle memory. And muscle memory is the key to proficiency--which equates to winning a confrontation--and is your only viable option.

Shot placement

Choosing where to place your shot is as important as proper shooting technique. So, before we discuss shot placement, we need a basic understanding of human anatomy.

The head

The human head is actually comprised of several plates of bone, which are fused together to create a helmet of sorts, under the skin of the scalp. Obviously, contained within the head, one will in most cases find a brain; this, however, does not by any means indicate that the individual has a mind, which is likely why he attacked you in the first place.

Surprisingly, a shot fired to the head will not *always* be effective. There are documented cases of individuals being shot in the head with center fire cartridges (9mm) where the projectile entered the skin of the scalp, but did not penetrate the cranium and were later removed by a simple excise of the scalp. And because there was no damage to the brain, the attacker was not immediately stopped or incapacitated, as was hoped.

If a shooter wishes to stop his attacker by using a shot to the head, there are very limited, specific areas which must be targeted to achieve the desired result. While there are several areas of the human skull which will likely cause immediate lethal damage and/or incapacitation, only a small number of those areas are appropriate for use within a defensive situation.

As a general rule the best place to fire a projectile at a human head is the area referred to as *the fatal triangle*. This area includes both eyes and the nose. This is because the eyes are connected to the brain via the optic nerve, which runs through a hole in the orbit, which is more commonly known as the *eye socket*. The bone of the orbit is very thin and is easily penetrated with minimal pressure. Therefore, any fast moving projectile introduced into this area can find a direct path to the brain. Additionally, the area located immediately behind the nose leads to sinus cavities, which also contain relatively thin layers of bone, protecting the inner cranium and brain. Because the brain is the hub of the central nervous system (CNS), any major trauma, either from blunt or direct penetration to this area, will likely cause immediate incapacitation; or at a minimum, confusion and disorientation, which will allow time for retreat. Due to the type of potential injury caused by a bullet to the head, the head and spine are considered *red zones*. (We will discuss the color-coding system a little later in this section).

The thoracic & abdominal cavities

The next area of the human body which we will discuss is referred to as the trunk or center of mass (COM). This includes the chest or thoracic cavity. Students of firearms weapon-craft are generally instructed to consider this the primary area of shot placement. Why? The answer to this question is actually quite simple: the COM is the largest target available. And the larger the target, the easier it is to hit. This is particularly relevant when one considers the accuracy degradation caused by extreme stress.

Now that we know why we aim for the COM, let's discuss what is contained in that area of the body. The COM of the human body is actually two separate areas. The first area is the top section and is referred to as the chest or thoracic cavity. This contains the major organs of the body. These include the heart, lungs, diaphragm, great vessels and the lower aspects of the throat structures including the trachea, larynx, and esophagus.

The following illustration represents the upper aspect of the COM also known as the thoracic region of the body and the major structures contained within.

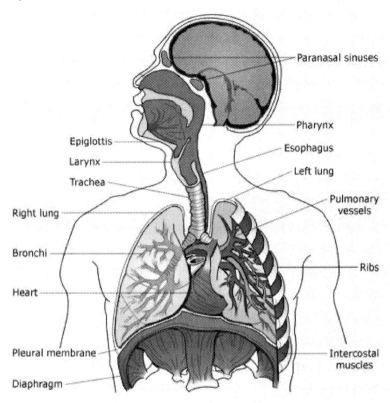

Whenever a significant amount of blunt trauma in the absence of penetrating trauma is presented to the heart, a disruption of the electrical impulses can be created which will cause what are referred to as *arrhythmias*. These can and in many cases will lead to death, if left untreated. Arrhythmias will occur whether the heart is penetrated or not, but in the case of physical penetration, they will be accompanied by profuse bleeding, which will often cause immediate incapacitation and death.

However, the heart is protected by a bone structure, known as the *sternum*, which allows for the potential deflection of a projectile unless significant energy is present behind the projectile. Still, even without penetration, a blunt trauma to the sternum will, in most cases, cause a secondary injury in the form of a cardiac arrhythmia as stated above.

So, rather than aim for the heart, you would be better off aiming for either side of the sternum, preferably the right. This is because the right side of the sternum is where the right lung is located. The right lung is the larger of the two lungs. When it collapses, it will cause additional strain on both the left lung and the heart. However, keep in mind that the human body is basically a redundant system. What this means is that although we have two lungs, only one lung is necessary for survival. Therefore, a projectile fired into the lung of an assailant should cause significant pain and bleeding but will not necessarily ensure immediate incapacitation. For this reason, an immediate retreat should be considered after the shot is fired.

Another consideration for shot placement is the throat wherein lies the *trachea,* or windpipe. A projectile presented to this area will immediately cause pain, profuse bleeding, and extreme difficulty in breathing. If an injury of this type is not attended to, it will cause imminent death due to either hemorrhagic shock, or possibly drowning in one's own blood.

This area should also be considered a *red zone* due to the potential of relatively rapid death and/or incapacitation should it be sufficiently damaged.

The next area of the COM we will discuss is known as the *abdominal cavity*. In the abdominal cavity we find the stomach, the liver, the spleen, the large and small intestines, A number of other blood vessels and smaller organs are also located deep within this area of the body.

The following illustration represents the lower aspect of the COM also known as the abdomen of the body and the major structures contained within.

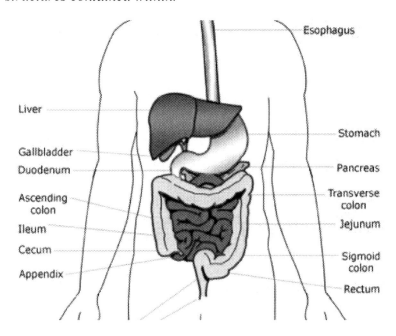

It should be noted, at this point, that while a foreign projectile presented to this area of the body will be extremely traumatic and will generally cause significant pain and profuse bleeding, this area of the body is considered a *yellow zone* due to the slower speed of full incapacitation. The general cause of death from injuries to this area include loss of blood or hemorrhagic shock, or will be related to a condition known as *sepsis* or septic shock, and is generally caused by the release of bacteria from a perforated bowel. Additionally, wounds to any of the organs contained within this region are extremely painful and will generally cause rapid incapacitation. However, if your assailant is under the influence of narcotics or excessive alcohol, these effects may be minimized and extreme caution should be exercised.

The extremities

The extremities of the body include the arms, legs, hands and feet. No vital organs, other than large blood vessels, are found in the extremities; therefore, these areas should be considered *green zones* due to the relatively slim chance that a projectile entering the extremities would cause either death or rapid incapacitation to an assailant. Additionally, due to the general size of these areas, they should never be considered a valid primary target because of the high miss probability.

The effects of a projectile on living tissue

Now that we have identified the various areas of the body, we will discuss exactly what occurs when a projectile penetrates the soft tissue of the body. The effects of a projectile on human tissue can be divided into two separate categories: blunt trauma and penetrating tissue disruption. In this section, we will examine both of these.

Blunt trauma is caused by the release of kinetic energy against a solid or semi solid object, causing the dispersion of energy against the target, and can be fatal, even in the absence of penetration. However, when a foreign projectile penetrates the body, the following occurs. First a *temporary wound channel* is created. Because the human body is mostly composed of water, the tissues and outer skin are extremely elastic in composition. This causes the body to act like self-sealing foam. Immediately upon entrance of the projectile, the blunt trauma and energy release of the projectile will cause the tissues to spread to avoid damage, thus creating the *temporary wound channel.* This is immediately followed by a return to their original shape, minus what is referred to as the *permanent wound channel.* This *permanent wound channel* is where bleeding occurs, causing additional injury to the tissue and internal structures of the body.

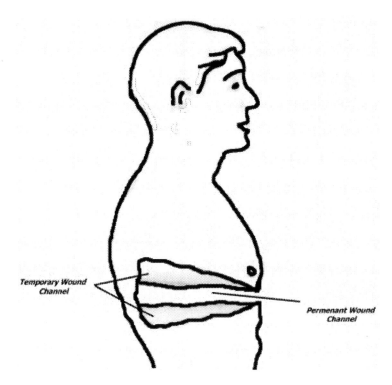

Temporary Wound Channel

Permenant Wound Channel

The illustration, above, depicts the effects of a projectile upon entering the body.

The objective of introducing a projectile into the body

When an individual makes the decision to use deadly force, it is assumed that the shooter will be acting in a defensive capacity, and the intention is not to kill the assailant, rather it is to stop their assailant from causing injury or death to themselves or someone else. That said, it is important to realize that there is no such thing as a "magic bullet" and that no caliber projectile is guaranteed to be 100% effective. This is where the color code system comes into consideration.

As stated above, damage to the areas of the human body referred to as *red zones* offer the highest probability of effectively killing or incapacitating an assailant quickly. A projectile fired into one of the areas referred to as *yellow zones*, while effective, will be less reliable for an immediate traumatic injury sufficient to cause death or incapacitation. This is not to say that a projectile fired into the abdomen of an attacker will not be effective, rather that a shot to this region of the body may not be *as* effective as a shot to the heart would be, because the projectile would not disrupt the tissues of either the main circulatory system or central nervous system.

We now move on to the least effective region of the human anatomy for the purpose of defensive shooting. The extremities are referred to as *green zones* because aside from the possibility of causing pain and eventual blood loss, these areas are difficult to hit while under extreme stress, and are not likely to cause the immediate incapacitation/death of your attacker.

Self-diagnosis of common shooting errors

It has always been my desire to impart to my students the ability to self-diagnose common shooting problems when they encounter them. In this section, we will discuss some of the more common problems and errors, as well as the methods and techniques that can be used to identify them and correct them.

One or two eyes open. Depending upon whom you ask, you will likely hear varying opinions as to whether it is better to shoot while keeping one or two eyes open. While it is better to try to keep both eyes open while engaging a target--as this allows for added ambient light to reach the optic nerves, reduces eye fatigue, and provides better depth perception--it is ultimately a matter of preference. There is no hard and fast rule which states that a shooter *must* use one or both eyes. In fact, some shooters display increased accuracy using only one eye.

But what about people who are right side master and left eye dominant? This is actually not a problem. When a shooter's dominant eye is opposite their master side, it simply requires a small variation in the positioning of the shooter's head.

While it may appear awkward and will cause the shooter to lower his chin, which could potentially impact accuracy, this can be overcome with training and practice. The most common problem encountered, by people whose master side and dominant eye are opposing each other, is the brass cases which tend to come back and hit them in the head as they are ejected from the chamber, after firing.

Anticipated Recoil. Anyone who has ever fired a firearm, has experienced *anticipated recoil.* Many will not admit that they have experienced it, but it is a phenomenon all new shooters encounter. It is characterized by a flinching reflex. While typically only a minor irritant, anticipated recoil can range from simply annoying to outright dangerous. It is annoying when you aim for a specific spot on a target and the shot impacts a few inches away from its desired location. The dangerous aspect of anticipated recoil is found when you aim for a specific location on the target and miss the target completely, endangering by-standers.

Anticipated recoil may be caused by a number of things, including poor follow through, problems with trigger control, and shooter apprehension.

To address the issue of poor follow through and trigger control I will generally instruct the student in the following technique, which has helped several of my students to overcome this problem. Here is the method I use:

☐ Start by using a traditional double action pistol.

☐ Next, chamber a *snap cap.* This a cartridge shaped object containing a spring and is designed for use during dry fire exercises, to protect the firing pin from advancing too far into the chamber and potentially causing damage to the firing pin, or other components of the action. (This will also serve to ensure that the weapon cannot be loaded with a live round).

☐ Place an empty cartridge case atop of the slide, just behind the front sight.

☐ Maintain a proper grip and stance as you press the trigger straight to the rear, in a smooth, continuous manner.

☐ The objective is to dry fire the weapon *without* the empty case falling off of the slide or barrel if using a revolver.

As for shooter apprehension, unfortunately there are only two methods of correction I am aware of. One is better than the other, as will be understood in a moment. The first technique is to downgrade the weapon caliber and continually practice until you begin to feel more comfortable and then gradually increase back to the caliber you began to experience the problem with.

The second technique, which I do not recommend, is to increase practice time and round counts with the caliber you are having a problem with. The theory here is that you will eventually overcome your apprehension. While you will eventually overcome this condition, you may also spend a significant amount of time and money developing bad habits which may cause problems later. These problems typically result from shooter discomfort and may not be immediately evident to the shooter. Therefore, if you should decide to use this approach, it should be done under the guidance and close supervision of an instructor to ensure proper technique is being used.

Combat vs. target shooting

When people are new to tactical shooting, it is not uncommon for them to become frustrated at what they perceive to be a dramatic reduction in accuracy as they attempt to increase their speed. At this point in a student's training, I like to explain that there is a big difference between target shooting and tactical, or defensive, shooting.

The objective with target shooting is to put all of the shots in the same hole or as close thereto as possible in the center of the target. In combat shooting, the objective is to hit a vital area, which will cause incapacitation and removal of the immediate threat. This is not to say that a tight group of shots in the area of choice is not desirable, rather that it is less important in tactical shooting than in target shooting and there are some cases in which it is actually beneficial if the shots are spaced further apart. This is because, as we discussed earlier, more damage can sometimes be done to an attacker if there are more wound channels created.

The following scenarios will demonstrate the reasons for what is stated above more clearly.

Scenario 1. Three shots are fired into the COM of an attacker. All three hits touch each other. While they are all located in a vital area of the body, none of the shots are sufficient to stop or incapacitate the attacker immediately.

And although the attacker is bleeding, all fluid loss is coming from a single hole.

Scenario 2. Three shots are fired into the COM of an attacker. All three hit in different places, about 2 or 3 inches from each other. While located in a vital area of the body, none of the shots are sufficient to stop or incapacitate the attacker immediately. And, as above, the attacker is bleeding; however, the fluid loss is now coming from multiple locations in the same region.

Of these two scenarios, the best scenario from the shooter's perspective is scenario 2. This is because in the second scenario there will be increased tissue damage and greater fluid loss due to multiple penetrations.

Another consideration is the element of time. Generally people who are new to combat shooting will require more time to place shots within a very tight group, and as such will often hesitate in an effort to ensure this effect. While this is not a problem in a controlled environment, such as a training course, it is important to remember that when an attack occurs, people who are trained will fall back on the training they have received. Therefore, it is important to train in scenarios that mimic a conflict situation as closely as possible and with as much simulated stress as can be applied.

The ready position

The term ready position describes the position in the shooter is in when the weapon is readily available for deployment, should the need arise. There are two specific forms of ready position.

The high ready position:

In the *high ready* position the weapon is grasped with either a one or two-handed grip and is held high up, close in the center of the chest, between the breast line with the muzzle canted at a downward angle. Due to the need to present the weapon in a straight and forceful manner, this technique is superior to the low ready position, which we will cover next.

The high ready position also allows the shooter to acquire sight alignment more quickly, as the amount of movement required to raise the weapon to eye level is significantly decreased. When deploying a pistol from the *high ready* position, the eyes of the shooter remain focused on the target and the weapon is thrust directly forward in the direction of the target. If performed correctly, the sights of the weapon will interrupt the line of sight between the shooter and the target, allowing for rapid and correct sight alignment. The *high ready* position should be used anytime an engagement is anticipated or between engagements, while scanning for additional threats.

There are two reasons for this:

1. The high ready position provides increased security as the weapon is kept close to the body.
2. The high ready position requires less movement to present the weapon against an attacker.

The low ready position:

In the *low ready* position the weapon is grasped in the same manner as with the *high ready* with one exception: the location against the body where the weapon is maintained. In the *high ready* position the weapon is maintained in the center of the chest at breast line; while in the *low ready* position the weapon is maintained against the lower abdomen. Both of these techniques are used in preparation for an attack, and both allow for the shooter to maintain the weapon at a state of readiness while still maintaining the ability to protect the weapon from obstructions.

Personally, I prefer not to use the *low ready* position for the following reasons.

1. The weapon is maintained too low against the body and leverage becomes a concern.

2. Additional, unnatural, movement is required to bring the weapon to proper sight alignment from the low ready position.

The following illustrations depict both the high ready and the low ready positions.

Handgun and Holster Selection

A common question among students of basic firearms-training courses, and a subject of much debate among instructors, is whether to buy a revolver or semi-automatic pistol. As important as this may seem, this is largely a matter of personal preference. Some instructors will be more interested in weapon size or a particular caliber. From my perspective, any choice must begin with your specific anatomical and self-protection requirements. Unless you understand these needs and know the right questions to ask, you should not depend on a local gun dealer to guide your choice. For one thing, they are in business to make money, so they may simply lead you to the most expensive weapon they think you will buy. Secondly, they are not *usually* professional instructors and their knowledge of self-protection tactics is, therefore, likely to be limited. The following guidelines will help you make a selection that will give you what you want and, more importantly, what you *need*.

Intended purpose

If you simply want to target shoot or "plink," then a .22 caliber may be your best choice. There is virtually no recoil, the ammunition is very inexpensive, and a .22 caliber is extremely accurate. If you need a pistol for home defense only, you likely won't be carrying the pistol, so weight and size are not major issues. However, a carry gun for self-defense raises important considerations. These include the size of the pistol, (so you can conceal it correctly), its weight (because you will be carrying it with you most of the time), the make (because you need the pistol to be reliable), and last, but certainly not least, the pistol's type of action and your ability to spend the required time *breaking in* the weapon. This process typically requires firing and average of 300 – 500 rounds.

Let's put these considerations to the test. We'll start by assuming you have decided to purchase a handgun for personal self-defense. To select the right pistol, you'll need to address the following areas.

Comfort and ergonomics

When a pistol fits properly, you'll be able to wrap your hand almost completely around the grip, with about three-quarters of an inch of open space on the other side of the grip. You will also be able to perform a two-handed grip without applying undue pressure with the fingers of your master side hand, and reach the trigger with your index finger without changing your gripping technique. And finally, you will be able to keep all of your fingers on the grip. If everything else about the fit is right, but your fingers hang off of the bottom of the grip, you may want a finger extension to will increase your hand comfort.

Concealability

In most areas where carrying a pistol is legal, the law states that the weapon must be concealed from the view of the general public. This can limit one's wardrobe. During the winter months, when most people wear heavy long coats, this is not much of an issue. But during the summer, it can be problematic. If you decide to carry your weapon with you, as opposed to using it solely for home defense, I suggest wearing a light shirt with long tails worn outside the pants. This will allow you the concealment you need even during warmer months. And even though it is still possible that some will suspect you are carrying a handgun, as long as your weapon is not clearly visible, you can comply with the law while maintaining your right to protect yourself.

However, the more critical task is finding the correct size pistol and the proper holster.

To help citizens exercising their concealed carry rights, most major handgun manufacturers are offering larger caliber pistols with smaller frames. These pistols provide the same degree of functionality as their full-sized counterparts, only in a smaller package. Heckler & Koch, for example, offers a series of USP 45acp semi-automatic handguns ranging from the full-sized model with a barrel length of approximately five inches to the compact with a 4-inch barrel.

Weight

Weight is another important criterion for any carry pistol. A handgun may not feel heavy when you first put it on, but remember, even the things we carry every day (briefcases, purses, books, backpacks) tend to weigh us down as the day rolls on. So, when choosing a pistol you plan to carry regularly, weight is a very important consideration. If you grow tired of carrying the extra weight, you will be more likely to stop carrying. What if you're attacked then? (Which, by the way, is the exactly when it's most likely to happen).

Quality

The saying, "you get what you pay for" applies here. You should expect to pay a minimum $400.00 – $500.00 for a quality pistol. And while I'll avoid specific recommendations, I believe it's generally best to stick with the major manufacturers.

The pistol you choose should be capable of taking *some* abuse. While I do not advocate testing this theory yourself, a handgun should be able to take a fall, from at least waist height, without resulting significant damage, or firing. Most manufacturers of quality arms will meet this criteria. Therefore, I again recommend sticking with a major manufacturer.

After all, a firearm is a tool, nothing more, and any tool is only as good as its strength and durability.

Weapon action

Recommending action types to novice students is a source of heated discussion among instructors. However, before we discuss why one action type is better than another, we need to understand the differences between them. And before we do that, we need to understand exactly what the *action* of a firearm is.

The action of a firearm is defined as "a group of moving parts which are designed to load, fire and unload a firearm." For our purposes, however, we will not be discussing the physical nomenclature of the action, rather we will go one step further and discuss the attributes and interactions between the parts of the various types of actions.

Single-action:

With a single-action weapon, the trigger is responsible for performing only one task: to release the hammer or striker allowing it to strike the firing pin and causing the weapon to fire. A classic example of a single-action firearm can be found in either the old western revolvers or the more modern 1911 weapon platforms, such as the Colt 45, which are both considered *semi-automatics*, as each time the trigger is engaged and the weapon is fired, the spent cartridge case is extracted and ejected and a new cartridge is loaded into the chamber, *automatically*.

With the single-action system, the hammer must be manually cocked prior to each firing. In the case of the western revolver, this would be accomplished either with the thumb or with a technique known as *fanning*. Fanning is often seen in Western movies and at shooting events. It involves aiming the muzzle of the weapon at the target, depressing the trigger and the repeatedly slapping the hammer, causing it to cock and release, thus firing the weapon. While with the semi-automatic, the action of the slide will often re-cock the hammer.

Traditional double-action:

With the traditional double-action weapon, the shooter has the choice of either simply pressing the trigger, which will cause the hammer to both cock and then release, allowing for the firing pin to be struck; or the hammer may be manually cocked and the trigger used to release the hammer only, as in the case of a single-action weapon.

It is important to remember that with a traditional double-action weapon, which is fired in the double-action mode, the amount of pressure required against the trigger will be different from the first to subsequent shots. This *can* cause accuracy problems, unless consistent practice is engaged in.

Double-action only:

The double-action only system is identical in every way to the traditional double-action with two exceptions: the hammer *cannot* be manually cocked, and the amount of trigger pressure needed to engage the hammer will be constant, similar to that of the single-action, except that it will be heavier.

Some instructors believe that single or double action does not matter. I counter this by saying that anyone unprepared to train, regularly, may have difficulty becoming accustomed to the safety features and trigger pressure required to fire a single-action pistol. A traditional double-action pistol is probably a better choice because you do not have to carry the pistol with the hammer cocked and the safety on at all times. With a double-action pistol, you need to simply draw, align the sights and press the trigger straight to the rear. Yes, the pressure required for the first shot is heavier than the subsequent shots, but with a little practice you'll become comfortable and proficient.

Calibers

Get a few gun people together and sooner or later the

discussion will turn to calibers and which one is best. For as long as manufacturers have produced different caliber weapons, gun owners have argued the issue. While I don't want to fuel the fire, I *can* help you make an informed decision based on your specific needs.

The term caliber is a measurement that describes the overall diameter of a projectile in relation to the bore (inside) of the gun barrel. To make matters more confusing, manufacturers use a couple of different formats to describe this calculation.

A 357 Magnum cartridge, for example, will have a projectile that is .357 hundredths of an inch (standard format). In contrast, the designation 9mm (9 millimeters) is a metric format for .355 hundredths of an inch.

Note: The difference between .357 hundredths of an inch and .355 may not appear like much. In fact, the energy transfer and power of each cartridge is significantly different due to the amount and type of powder charge found within each cartridge.

Here is a quick listing of common caliber sizes: 10mm, 45acp, .357 Magnum, 40 S&W, 9mm, and .22 caliber. Velocity and penetration power will further vary among cartridge brands and the handguns (different rifling and barrel lengths) from which they are fired.

Now for the controversy: among those who carry, shoot and train with handguns, many argue that the bigger the bullet, the better the stopping power. While this argument has some merit, it is far from the final word, especially in terms of each person's selection. Let's examine the issues that must be considered in choosing your weapon's caliber.

First, let's revisit our discussion regarding the purpose of using a weapon to target a body. The purpose is to create a series of anatomical and physiological effects on the body that will cause the recipient to cease his aggressive behavior. In less gentle terms, the projectile should deliver as much bodily trauma and tissue disruption as possible, producing as much blood loss as possible, causing the aggressor to become so weak, or incapacitated, that he no longer poses a threat; thus, enabling the person who is defending against the attack to escape.

Almost every defensive firearms trainer teaches students to aim for the COM first and the head or other area second. They don't advise going for the leg, arm or head initially because even a shooter who is extremely accurate in the controlled environment of the firing range will increase his odds of missing a smaller target when subjected to the stress of an actual attack. Only a highly trained professional should even consider such a shot; which, *if missed,* could injure or kill an innocent bystander. So, we train to aim for the COM, which includes the human thoracic and abdominal cavities (chest and abdomen) and contains 99% of the vital organs. Disruption to any of these organs will have a physiological effect, including the immediate loss of blood.

Another way of explaining this is to look at the effects of a projectile on living tissue. Remember, when a bullet enters the flesh it creates two channels. The first is the temporary wound channel: when the initial penetration occurs, initial release of energy transferred by the projectile causes the tissue to spread out of the way. The second is the permanent wound channel: after the initial energy has dissipated, a permanent wound channel remains, through which bleeding occurs.

If one projectile enters the body, creating a wound channel, the effects of that projectile will be determined by the caliber and type of bullet. By contrast, two or more projectiles will create additional wounds channels and will increase bleeding significantly. This will lead to quicker incapacitation.

For example, two 45acp rounds to the COM will cause a significant amount of damage to the human body, as will three or four 9mm cartridges.

The size of the initial channel, therefore, is directly related to the immediate energy transfer and displacement into the target and the tearing of tissue it creates.

Let's assume that a woman decides to purchase a handgun for self-defense. She visits a local gun store and explains to a salesperson that she has *never* fired a handgun before and only wants something for self-defense. The store clerk, who is of the "bigger is better" school of thought, sells her on a 45acp single-action pistol. She takes the pistol and proceeds to the local shooting range to try it out. After a quick overview, safety briefing, and instructions on how to load the pistol's magazine, a target is set up and she begins shooting.

Her accuracy is poor, but this is to be expected. She's never shot before. After a few shots, her hand begins to hurt. The gun is not comfortable. This is a serious problem because if she's not comfortable with the gun, she will not practice with it. And if she does not practice with it, she will not achieve proficiency.

So what are her options? She can try to force herself to practice until she becomes comfortable. However, this is unlikely to be successful simply due to the discomfort she will feel. On the other hand, she *could* trade it in on a smaller-caliber handgun such as a .22 caliber, which (with a well-placed shot) can be just as effective, and as lethal, as a .44 Magnum.

Shot placement is the critical key to effective defensive shooting, and your ability to control the recoil and minimize the reset time after a shot is fired enables you to place a second shot with equal accuracy. With proper training, and regular practice, anyone can learn to fire the larger calibers with a fair to high-degree of accuracy, speed and control. Unfortunately, most people either cannot or will not pursue the necessary training, nor engage in the required practice time needed to become comfortable with a large caliber handgun. The best solution, therefore, is to work, train and practice with a smaller caliber.

Now, let me clarify: while I said that a well-placed .22

caliber would be effective, I *do not* advocate using anything *less* than 9mm for personal defense. There are just too many variables that come into play during a violent defensive confrontation. This is because a 9mm is still relatively easy to handle and will *generally* cause enough significant tissue damage, if the proper area of the body is impacted and the appropriate defensive ammunition is used.

Additionally, virtually everyone can fire a 9mm and quickly regain control of the pistol for an immediate second shot. What's more the popularity of the 9mm has led to a decline in ammunition costs, which makes regular training and practice more affordable.

Now before any of you large bore readers start yelling, let me say that although I generally like the 9mm for the average user, I am not suggesting that it is the ultimate caliber. My recommendation is based on the fact that most people cannot and will not practice sufficiently to become proficient with larger calibers. I personally like the 45acp as a primary weapon, and a 9mm as a back up.

In conclusion, the best caliber for self-defense is the one that the individual can control effectively and reliably. And here is a final thought: Recall the attempted assassination of President Reagan. John Hinckley used a .22 caliber pistol. He almost killed the president and permanently injured Press Secretary James Brady. *The size of the projectile does not matter; the magic is in its placement.*

Holsters

In many cases, choosing the correct holster can be just as important as choosing the correct handgun. In this section I will provide you with my professional opinion on some of the more common and interesting types of holsters as well as provide you with my professional recommendations.

Fanny packs:

Although fanny packs are referred to by a variety of colorful names they do have a place, and if used correctly, and with the proper training, they are an excellent option. There are, however, some considerations which must be taken into account before the decision to use this type of holster is made. These considerations include the following:

☐ The user *must* receive training in the proper deployment of a pistol from the fanny pack, as the drawing techniques required are different than those used with a standard waist level holster. Without the proper training and practice, the time required to draw the weapon could have severe consequences.

☐ As with all things related to firearms and training, this next consideration is an area of debate. However, I believe that whenever possible one should refrain from using a black fanny pack, as it is almost always an indication to others, that a weapon is contained therein.

Inseam holsters:

Inseam holsters, which have been around for some time, require the weapon to be placed down the front of the wearer's pants, in the area of their inseam. While I will not discuss the specific problems I anticipate with this technique of carry (I would rather leave that to the imagination), I will say that I am completely opposed to this method of carry and the holster systems which utilize it.

Shoulder holsters:

While it is true that a shoulder holster will generally allow for easier concealment, they also cause the wearer to engage in excessive movement while drawing the weapon. This can lead to increased risk because of the increased time needed to present the weapon against the attacker. Therefore, as with fanny packs, it is recommended that anyone who intends to use a shoulder holster engage in professional training with a competent instructor.

Traditional hip holsters:

As stated earlier, traditional hip style holsters including "in the pants" holsters, can be positioned in different ways. This includes positioning the holster in front of the hip (*pelvic carry*) or behind the hip (*kidney carry*). I believe that this method of carry is the best method of carry, as it generally provides the greatest ability to protect the weapon. The only exception to this, would be with the *small of the back carry* which is the most comfortable method of carry, but which will reduce the ability to protect the weapon from an attacker's grasp unless you have been trained specifically in this area.

Another often neglected consideration with hip style holsters, is the use of the safety or security strap. It is accepted practice that if the holster has such a strap it *must* be used. If you do not wish to use it, you should remove it completely or choose another type of holster. Failure to abide by this rule can cause undesired problems to occur. One such problem is *printing,* which is to say that your weapon will be visible to an onlooker. And if it is the police who notice, you could loose your permit or license to carry.

Ankle holsters:

Ankle holsters are specialized holster systems which require training if they are to be used correctly and effectively. I personally use this type of holster system, depending on what I am doing at the time.

The proper way to use an ankle holster involves placing the device on the support side ankle of the body, which requires a cross draw scenario. It is for this reason that I strongly oppose the use of this holster system to maintain a primary weapon. Additionally, the use of an ankle holster system will generally require the modification of one's wardrobe, as the pant leg under which the weapon will be maintained must be significantly loose, to allow for immediate access.

Tactical leg holsters:

In my opinion, the most comfortable and effective holster system available is the tactical *drop rig* or tactical leg holster. Originally designed for special operations personnel to allow for immediate access from any position, these holsters are frequently used by instructors, law enforcement personnel and security personnel. Unfortunately, with this holster system, concealment is not a readily available option.

Drawing from the holster

Perhaps one of the most important principles of combat shooting is the ability to draw the weapon from its holster. While there are several techniques that can be used to draw a weapon from its holster, all of which rely heavily on the location in which the weapon is being carried on the body, the overall mechanics of the draw remain the same.

We will discuss the mechanics of drawing from a holster as they apply to the carrying of a handgun on the crest of the ilium, or hip. There are two carrying positions we will be working with: the *kidney carry* and the *pelvic carry*. In both of these positions the holster is worn near the crest of ilium. However, in the *pelvic carry* mode the weapon is in front of the hip and in the *kidney carry* position it is placed behind the hip.

For many people, the *kidney carry* position is more comfortable as the weapon does not generally dig into the body while seated, as it is prone to do with the *pelvic carry* position.

REMEMBER: Before attempting any of the drills listed herein, it is absolutely imperative that you must abide by all of the safety rules and protocols I have outlined. This means ALWAYS make sure that your weapon is unloaded. And ALWAYS check it at least three times.

A student and friend who has been with me for quite a few years, is fond of telling a story of a training technique I used on him. Although it's a very simple technique, it works quite well.

The first thing I did was demonstrate the drawing technique I wanted him to learn. Then I had him practice it in my presence several times until I was sure he had it down. I then told him that I wanted him to go home, and after ensuring that the weapon was unloaded by checking a minimum of *3* times, I wanted him to continue to practice drawing the weapon at the same speed he was using at this point, for 20 minutes a day, three to four times per week. I asked him to keep this up until we were scheduled to meet again, in two weeks.

When he returned to the range, he demonstrated that his skill had dramatically improved, as had his speed. Later, when he described this technique to a new student, he admitted that at first he was thought it was a waste of time. But being prior career military, he was accustomed to following instructions, so he did as he was told. In the end, he was quite pleased with the results.

The reason for the improvement he experienced is directly related to the development of muscle memory and the reinforcement of a specific skill. This is why it is so important to practice regularly--even if you think you've already mastered a specific skill. Here is the technique I used.

The 5-point draw

1. The master hand moves to secure a firm grip on the weapon and releases the safety/security strap, while the support hand moves to the center of the torso and waits.

2. The weapon is drawn from the holster while canting the muzzle forward, causing the front sight and muzzle to snap forward when cleared from the holster.

3. Once clear of the holster, the butt of the weapon is moved across the front of the body, held as closely to the body as possible, until it meets the support hand in the center of the torso where a two-handed grip is performed.

4. Both arms are extended forward in the direction of the target.

5. The sights are aligned and the weapon is discharged, if necessary.

The following series of illustrations, above, depicts the 5-point draw in sequence.

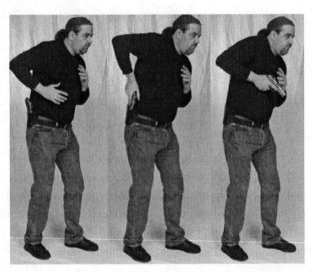

Reloads, stoppage clearing and press checks:

In this section, we will address the three types of reload techniques as well as the three most common types of malfunctions/stoppages. Additionally, we will discuss the most common method for clearing a stoppage and when and how this technique should be applied. While some of these techniques are difficult to master, they are absolutely critical skills for anyone who owns and carries a handgun.

Before learning or practicing the various reloading techniques, it is important to ensure that your equipment (such as magazine pouches) are correctly positioned, and that the magazines contained within are correctly inserted and ready for use. Just like a hip style holster, either a single or double magazine pouch can be carried on the belt in either the kidney or pelvic carry modes. In either case, it is important that the magazines be inserted correctly into their respective slots.

The correct method of maintaining the magazines is to ensure that the cartridges are facing forward, in the direction of the target. This is to ensure that when you move to retrieve a magazine from the holder you grasp it correctly, with your finger aligned along the front of the magazine which will aid in a faster insertion into the weapon's magazine well.

NOTE: The act of reloading a weapon should always be performed when the shooter wants *to reload, never when the shooter* needs *too. This means that whenever possible, reload before the magazine is empty. Of course, it is not always possible to reload before you run out of bullets, so we will also cover a reloading technique designed to be used when the weapon is fired until it is empty.*

The speed reload:

The first reloading technique we will discuss is known as the *speed reload.* The speed reload is perhaps the most common reloading technique and is used by most shooters.

The basic principles of the *speed reload* involve releasing the magazine of the semi-automatic pistol and allowing it to simply fall to the ground. The primary advantage of the *speed reload* is that by simply allowing the magazine to drop to the ground, the support hand is left free to more rapidly assume the proper grip and begin shooting again. In addition to being a quicker reload technique, the *speed reload* is also the easiest reloading technique.

The *speed reload* is performed as follows:

☐ First, make sure you are positioned in an area of concealment or cover. (Cover is best, but if unavailable, concealment will do).

☐ Move your weapon to the high ready position with your master hand and use your support hand to retrieve a spare magazine.

☐ To ensure a proper grip on the fresh magazine, make sure the pointer finger of the support hand is indexed along the front of the magazine, just below the first round. This is done to ensure that the magazine is properly aligned for insertion and will assist in the proper placement of the fresh magazine.

- [ ] After getting the proper grip on the fresh magazine, move it from its holder to the weapon.

- [ ] When the fresh magazine is within two or three inches of the weapon, depress the magazine release on the weapon and allow the used magazine to fall to the ground.

- [ ] Insert the fresh magazine and seat it into the magazine well, by striking in a upwards motion against the floor plate of the magazine.

- [ ] Then your support hand is rotated back to its proper grip position, allowing for the weapon sights to be reacquired and the weapon to be discharged.

The following illustration demonstrates the speed reload.

The tactical reload:

The *tactical reload* is a more complicated technique and will require more practice to achieve proficiency. The primary difference between the *tactical reload* and the *speed reload* (as well as the *emergency reload*, which will be discussed next) is that with the *tactical reload* the magazine is held in the support hand while additional shots are fired. When the shooter stops shooting, the magazine is secured in the pocket or waistband of the shooter.

The primary advantage of the *tactical reload* is in the shooter's ability to retain both the fresh magazine and any additional cartridges remaining in the used magazine, when moving from one cover position to another.

The *Tactical Reload* is performed as follows:

- [ ] As with the *speed reload*, the shooter should be in a position of concealment, at a minimum, and preferably, cover.

- [ ] The weapon is brought to the high ready position with the master hand while the support hand moves to retrieve a spare magazine.

- [ ] The support hand obtains a proper grip on the fresh magazine, which includes positioning the pointer finger of the support hand so that it is indexed along the front of the magazine, just below the first round contained in the magazine. (Again, this is done to ensure that the magazine is properly aligned for insertion, and will assist in the proper placement of the fresh magazine).

- [ ] The fresh magazine is removed from the holder or other storage area and moved to the weapon.

- [ ] When the fresh magazine is within two or three inches of the weapon, the used magazine should be released from the weapon by depressing the magazine release while retrieving it between the fingers of the support hand.

- [ ] The fresh magazine is then inserted and seated in the magazine well, by striking in a upwards motion against the floor plate of the magazine

- [ ] The support hand is rotated back into the proper grip position, allowing for the weapon sights to be reacquired and for the weapon to be discharged.

The following illustration demonstrates the tactical reload.

The emergency reload:

The third technique we will discuss is the *emergency reload*. The *emergency reload* technique is similar to the *speed reload* in that the old magazine is released and allowed to fall to the ground. However, with the *emergency reload* the weapon is fired until it is empty and the slide is locked in the open position. This requires the insertion of a fresh magazine, as well as the additional action of releasing the slide in order to allow the cartridge to be chambered.

Due to the extra step required, it is considered the *least* desirable reloading technique. A simple concept which will assist you in avoiding the need to use this reloading technique is to reload when you *want* to, not when you *have* to.

And please remember that *all* of the reloading techniques described herein should be learned and practiced while under the direct supervision of a qualified instructor, to ensure that the techniques are performed properly and safely.

The performance of the *emergency reload* is identical to that of the *speed reload*, with the exception of two additional steps.

The technique is performed as follows:

☐ The shooter should be positioned in a area of at minimum, concealment, but preferably cover.

133

- [ ] The weapon is moved to the high ready position with the master hand, while the support hand moves to retrieve a spare magazine.

- [ ] Once the support hand has obtained a proper grip on the fresh magazine, which includes positioning the pointer finger of the support hand along the front of the magazine, just below the first round contained in the magazine. (Again, this is done to help ensure that the magazine is properly aligned for insertion and will assist in the proper placement of the fresh magazine).

- [ ] The magazine is then removed from the holder or other storage area and moved to the weapon.

- [ ] After the fresh magazine is within two to three inches of the weapon, release the used magazine by depressing the magazine release and allowing it to fall to the ground.

- [ ] Insert the fresh magazine into the magazine well and seat it by striking in a upwards motion against the floor plate of the magazine, and close the slide by pulling it back slightly with the support hand to disengage the slide stop, which will allow the slide to strip off a round from the magazine, load the cartridge into the chamber, and slide to lock in position.

- [ ] Rotate the heel of the support hand back over the thumb of the master hand and re-establish your two-handed grip.

The following illustration demonstrates the emergency reload.

All of the steps above should be performed as quickly as possible, with one exception: when you eject and replace the magazines, be careful.

If done too quickly, you may cause the magazine to be seated improperly and that can lead to a weapon malfunction.

Stoppages and malfunctions:

A firearm is a mechanical device and as such is inherently prone to malfunctions, such as stoppages and failures. As with any other mechanical device, there are multiple reasons for this. In this section, we will discuss the most common types of malfunction and the accepted methods of addressing them.

Failure to feed

This malfunction is caused when the cartridge is not properly loaded into the chamber. This can be the result of poor gripping techniques, such as *limp wristing*. This happens when the grip on the weapon is not up high enough on the backstrap. This presents a problem because the weapon must cycle properly in order to reload between shots, and if the weapon is held too low on the backstrap, the shooter's hand can interfere with this cycling motion, as the weapon is not allowed to cycle straight to the rear.

Other problems can occur if your weapon is damaged in any way. For example, if you have bent feed lips on the magazine or an excessive build up of debris in the weapon's action.

The double feed

The double feed occurs when the cartridge is not fully ejected from the weapon and a new round is stripped from the magazine, leaving two cartridges wedged in the weapon chamber. This type of malfunction can be also be caused by *limp wristing* as the weapon is not allowed to fully cycle.

The following illustration demonstrates the double feed

The stove pipe stoppage

The stovepipe condition occurs when the expended case fails to eject completely from the weapon and becomes caught between the top of the barrel and the breach face of the slide. This causes the case to stick straight up from the top of the weapon, giving it the appearance of a stovepipe. Some of the causes of this type of malfunction include worn or damaged magazines, out of sync timing, burrs or unpolished surfaces on the chamber's feed ramp, bent or damaged extractors, damaged/malformed bullets or shooter error caused by poor technique, including *limp wristing.*

The following illustration demonstrates the stovepipe stoppage.

Failure to fire

The failure to fire is often caused by an ammunition flaw. Although it can be caused by a weapon malfunction, it is more commonly caused by a problem with the cartridge itself.

However, if the firearm is at fault, the cause may be damage to, or breakage of, the firing pin. It may also be the result of an improperly seated magazine, which will prevent a cartridge from being properly loaded into the chamber. Additional causes of a failure to fire may include something referred to as *hard primers.* This is where the firing pin strikes the primer but there is insufficient force to cause the primer to ignite. A failure to fire may also be caused by contamination of the internal powder charge, which may have come in contact with some form of outside chemical.

Stoppage clearing:

In the end, what matters most during a violent confrontation is not what caused the stoppage or malfunction, but what you can do about it. Failure to act appropriately and quickly can lead to disastrous results. In this section, we will discuss the fastest and most accepted methods of clearing a stoppage.

The technique I'm about to describe is known by two names: the *tap, rack, bang* technique and the *tap, rack, assess, engage* technique. Regardless of the name used to describe it, it is the fastest and most efficient method of clearing a stoppage.

☐ The first step in performing this technique is to point the weapon in a safe direction (or in the direction of a hostile target) and strike the weapon in an upwards motion against the magazine base with the heel of the palm of your support hand. This will ensure that the magazine is completely and properly seated within the magazine well.

☐ The next step is to reach over and grasp the rear portion of the top of the weapon's slide, avoiding the muzzle and the breach, and pull (rack) the slide rearward, ejecting any cartridge which may have been lodged within the chamber. Then allow the slide to cycle forward, loading a fresh cartridge into the chamber.

☐ The third and final step in this technique is to reacquire a proper grip, align the sights and discharge the weapon, if necessary.

The following illustration better demonstrates the technique described, above.

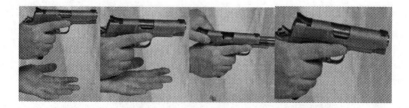

This technique can be used for any of the stoppages listed in this section and, like all the techniques in this book, should be practiced, regularly, to maintain proficiency.

The time to think about stoppage clearing is, as with all defensive techniques, *before* you actually need it. For when engaged in a conflict, failure to react quickly and automatically can have disastrous consequences.

Dead chambers

Although a dead chamber is not technically a stoppage, carrying a firearm with a dead or "cold" chamber can have the same potentially deadly effect. Therefore, in this section, we will be covering this situation as well.

In my years as an instructor in firearms and tactics, I have always made a conscious effort to avoid arguing with students. I also do my best to avoid arguing with potential students, regular shooters and gun store commandoes.

But there comes a time when an issue is simply too important to ignore. One such issue is the often touted practice of carrying an unloaded gun.

When I ask people who practice this habit why they carry an unloaded weapon, they pretty much always say the same thing: they carry an unloaded gun because they're afraid if they carry a loaded gun, it will accidentally fire. Here's the problem: *if it isn't loaded, it can't protect you.* It's really that simple. If you want to avoid accidents, practice good firearms training. Don't wander around with an unloaded weapon. The only thing an unloaded weapon will do is create a bulge in your silhouette--it won't protect you. If your purpose in buying and carrying a handgun is self-protection, the weapon must be loaded. Granted, if you have plenty of time to load your weapon before an attack, your weapon could still end up providing protection, but how do you know that you will have time? *You don't, and in all likelihood won't.*

If this concerns you, here's some factual information that might put you at ease. With old-style western single action revolvers from the 19th century, for example, the hammer always rested on a dead chamber.

This was because the weapons of that time lacked any internal safety features. This is not the case today. With modern technologies, the chances of a weapon firing accidentally are significantly reduced.

Here's an exercise you can practice if you're still feeling a uncomfortable about carrying a loaded weapon. But keep in mind: ***GREAT CAUTION MUST BE USED WHEN PEFORMING THE FOLLOWING EXERSIZE.***

Step 1: Begin by having either your spouse, girlfriend, boyfriend, lover, friend, etc. take possession of two of your magazines.

Step 2: Have this person load one magazine with live ammunition, and the other magazine with training or dummy rounds.

Step 3: After this is done, have this other person load the weapon for you, tap the magazine into the weapon to make sure it is firmly inserted and apply tape around the slide and the butt of the grip to prevent you from inspecting the weapon's chamber or magazine contents. The weapon should then be placed down on the table and retrieved by you. *Do not accept the weapon with the action closed.* Remember you *may* be dealing with live ammunition.

Step 4: After you have picked up the weapon, place it in your holster and proceed to carry it around the house. Perform this technique every day for a week or so. Make sure the person loading the weapon is alternating the magazines without your knowledge. Since you will never know if the weapon you are carrying has live ammunition or plastic training rounds in it, after a while, the natural anxiety from carrying the weapon with the chamber loaded *should* pass.

Warning: It cannot be overstated that this training drill should NEVER be attempted or practiced on the street, and should only be attempted within a controlled environment where the likelihood of attack is at a minimum.

Press checks:

The term *press check* is used to describe a technique for verifying the condition of the chamber in a semi-automatic pistol. This technique is extremely important to practice and make a part of your regular routine whenever you handle a weapon. I teach my students that any time a weapon is loaded, reloaded or retrieved from a location away from its holster (i.e. a table, etc.), a *press check* should be performed.

Performing a press check

While there are several different ways to perform a press check, we will only discuss the two most common methods. Of these two, one is recommended; while the other is not. This is because the second method violates safety protocols and will only work with a limited number of weapon types. However, since both are common, we will cover them both.

The wrong way to perform a press check

The first method, and the one I do *not* recommend, was developed by soldiers using the 1911 pistol during WWII. This requires placing the finger or hand in front of the muzzle and putting the thumb inside the trigger guard.

This technique will only work with a 1911 style weapon or something similar, which does not contain a full-length guide rod.

To perform this type of *press check*, you must grip the weapon with your master hand while placing the thumb of the support hand inside the master trigger guard while the index finger of the same hand is placed in front of the weapon, just under the muzzle. Then you push the slide to the rear of the weapon while you inspect the breach of the weapon to determine whether or not there is a cartridge within the chamber.

The following illustration depicts the incorrect method of performing the press check described above and is NOT recommended.

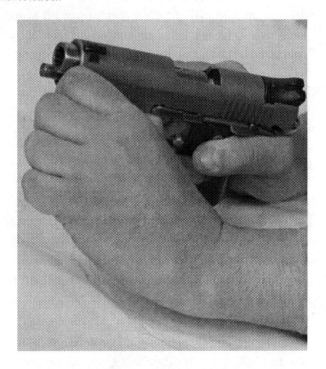

The correct way to perform a press check

The correct way to perform a press check and the method I teach to all my students, is as follows:

While maintaining the muzzle in a safe and appropriate direction with the master hand, the rear of the weapon's slide is grasped on either side and the weapon is turned slight back toward you to allow for a clearer view of the breach. The slide is pulled back slightly, exposing the inside of the chamber.

The following illustration depicts the preferred method of performing a press check.

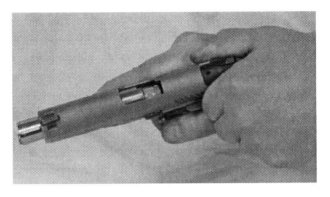

Many manufacturers have redesigned their weapons with loaded chamber indicators, peepholes or other methods of determining the condition of the chamber, to permit visualization of the chamber without requiring a *press check*. However, I still insist that all of my students learn the correct method of checking a chamber for the following reasons:

☐ Some weapons will not be designed with these relatively new features.

☐ As with any mechanical feature, there is always a possibility of failure.

☐ In the middle of a violent conflict, or low-light environment, the need to search for a relatively small hole to indicate a weapon's status can, and often will, take longer than is acceptable.

For these reasons you should always perform a *press check* whenever a weapon is loaded, reloaded or retrieved from a location outside of your immediate control. This includes any time the weapon has been removed from its holster or returned from another user.

Controlled pairs and hammers

The term *double tap* is an often over used and misunderstood phrase, so in this section, I will explain exactly what the term means, and when and how the technique should be applied. To begin with, the term *double tap* refers to a shooting technique in which two rounds are fired in rapid succession. However the term is a misnomer, as it actually describes two separate and very distinct shooting techniques. The first of these is the hammer.

The Hammer:

The *hammer* is performed by aligning the sights on the target once and engaging the trigger twice, in rapid succession. Due to the nature of a *hammer*, it is a considerably faster technique than the *controlled pair*, which we will discuss, below. However, because you will only align your sights on the target once, you need to be close enough to the target to ensure that the second shot will also engage the target and not deviate excessively from the target area due to the recoil of the weapon.

The Controlled Pair:

The *controlled pair* is the firing of two rounds in rapid succession; however before *each* shot is fired, the sights of the weapon are aligned on the target. Although performed rapidly, the *controlled pair* is a slower and more precise method of firing two rapid shots than the *hammer*.

Whenever a pistol is drawn in a violent confrontation, it is assumed that you are authorized to use deadly force. So we need to quickly revisit what the intention of firing the weapon is. Is it to scare the hostile? No. Is it to wound the hostile? No. Is it to kill the hostile? No. The intention of discharging a firearm at another human being during a violent encounter is to *stop* the hostile from presenting a threat to you.

And the fastest way to stop an aggressive attack, is to fire two initial rounds at the largest target available, which will be the COM of your attacker.

Now, let's say we need to stop an aggressor who is approximately 18 feet away. Do we use a *controlled pair* or a *hammer*? Give up? Well, if you said a *hammer*, sorry but you are wrong. At a distance of 18 feet or more, you are more likely to hit your target with two well placed shots if you use a *controlled pair*.

Remember, distance will change the angle of the shot even with a *controlled pair*. During a high stress situation, such as an attack, you cannot expect to put two rounds in the same hole, nor should you want to, as the objective of the bullet is to create as much tissue damage as possible; thus causing the hostile threat to either stop or retreat. So, a *controlled pair* should be used for any distance beyond 10 to 12 feet; whereas, a *hammer* should be used for anything closer.

Cover vs. concealment

Understanding the difference between cover and concealment is critical within a tactical engagement. The term concealment means simply to "conceal from view." However, it must be understood that concealment will *not* provide any level of effective ballistic protection.

For examples of concealment, place yourself in a scenario where you are being attacked by someone with a gun. You are armed and have drawn your pistol while heading for anything which will block you from your attacker's view. Your choices are a Rubbermaid garbage can, a car or a bush. Which object will be cover and which object will be concealment? Well, the garbage can and bush are forms of concealment; while the car is a form of cover. Why? Because neither the garbage can nor the bush will stop or even sufficiently slow down a projectile. Will these objects hide you from the *view* of your attacker? Yes, they will. But they will offer you no actual physical or ballistic protection. So, now we move onto cover.

Cover is defined as any object, which *will* afford the user a degree of ballistic protection. Examples of cover objects are cars, dumpsters, trees, and mailboxes, etc. Why? Because these objects contain sufficient mass to slow down, or perhaps even stop, a projectile.

Now that we have determined what cover and concealment are, we can move on to the proper use of these principles. To begin with, we need to refresh our memories with regard to situational awareness: when out in public, pay attention to your surroundings. This does not mean that you should walk around thinking that there is a terrorist behind every corner; however, you should be mindful of your surroundings and continually search to identify locations of cover/concealment for use, *if* a violent confrontation were to develop.

Consider the following scenario. You are walking out of the mall when you see two gang-bangers arguing. You are carrying your weapon but you decide to skirt to the left to avoid them. You see a garbage can and a pillar immediately to your left about 10 feet away. Next thing you know, these two fine upstanding citizens draw their guns and start shooting at each other and *you*. What is the first thing you should do? Do you draw your pistol and start blasting away? No. You do not. The first thing you should do is move in the direction the nearest cover while drawing your weapon and preparing for combat.

Now, you are behind your cover. How should you position yourself? Well, for one thing, do not pretend you are in the movies where you hug the side of your cover position, as this action will cause your movements to be restricted and could present a serious problem. Instead, use the following list as a guide for properly using cover and/or concealment.

Using cover:

The use of cover is not a hard principle to learn; however, it does require adherence to some simple steps:

☐ Position yourself two or three feet behind your cover object, to allow for free movement.

☐ Whenever possible, crouch in a kneeling position, as this makes you as small a target as possible.

☐ Wait and watch until the situation ends on its own, the police arrive, or you are forced to engage the target.

Now, if you must engage the target, which means that you have no safe avenue of retreat and your life is in imminent danger, there is a series of protocols which must be adhered to at all times.

These protocols include the following:

☐ Do not ever expose yourself from behind your cover for more than 2 or 3 seconds. If you cannot acquire proper sight alignment and engage the target within that three second limit, immediately return to cover and wait to try again.

☐ Another important principle is balance. When you come out from behind cover, and are attempting to obtain a proper sight picture, you will need to be balanced. This means both feet should be on the ground in a way that keeps you stable. If you are unbalanced, you will take more time than you have to obtain your sight acquisition and the results could be fatal. Remember, time is as much your enemy or greater as is your attacker.

☐ If you need to move out and back to cover repeatedly, the quickest way to do this is to pivot back and forth. To do this, your support leg should rotate out while you pivot on your master foot.

☐ A quick peek, while staying mostly covered, is also a good technique. If you keep your body behind the object providing cover and simply poke your head out quickly, you can pull back right away and avoid becoming a target, while still gaining information as to your attacker's position.

Movement within a violent confrontation:

The very action of movement within a violent confrontation is wrought with hazards. These include an increased exposure to the threat, the potential for tripping over a foreign object or other obstacles, and the possibility (when acting as part of a team or group) of stumbling into the area of control of another person. In fact, with all of these potential problems, you may be wondering why not just stay put? The reason is that there are times when movement will be required, and it is at these times that the principle of proper balance can mean the difference between life, death, and/or injury.

Proper tactical movement cannot be learned completely through any book or video, as I have stated in earlier sections. However, it is possible to learn principles which will assist the participant when formal training is engaged in.

While there are actually several specific classifications of movement within the realm of the defensive arts, in this section I will focus only on the basic principles, in an effort to provide an overview from which to encourage you to pursue further with a qualified instructor.

Balance—As stated above, balance is the key. To ensure proper balance while moving, both feet should be maintained flat on the ground whenever you are not moving. In other words, whenever you stop, make sure both feet are flat on the ground. The slightest elevation of the heel of either foot can cause the body to be out of alignment, and therefore, off balance.

The Eyes—We all have eyes, and it is important to use them. When considering whether to move from one position to another, it is imperative that you do a quick scan of the area for potential obstacles which may be in your way. The downside, of course, is that by do in this, your eyes are removed from the threat. So, if possible, try to visualize your surroundings prior to moving, or better yet, develop a mental picture of your surroundings *before* the confrontation begins. Two words . . . SITUATIONAL AWARENESS!!!!! When you enter an area, do not only look for potential threats, but also look for potential cover or concealment and the obstacles between them.

Speed—Speed during tactical movement is also of great importance. But your speed must take into account the terrain you are dealing with. For example, if you are in a flat parking lot or similar location, it is unlikely that you will encounter many obstacles which you will not be able to see, and therefore you should be able to move quickly. If, however, the terrain is a field or similar with grass, etc. there could be obstructions which are not immediately visible, and therefore additional caution must be exercised. Your physical condition must be taken into account as well.

Style—The style of movement one should engage in when attempting to escape a violent conflict, or move from one position of cover to another, will also be largely dependant upon the situation. The following list covers the main styles of tactical movement:

☐ *Covert or Stealth*—This style of movement is used when there is a need to maintain the element of surprise. This type of movement is very slow and deliberate and each step is considered beforehand in an effort to reduce the chance of excessive noise.

☐ *Warrant*—This style of movement is actually a rapid jog or half-run style, which involves moving at a higher rate of speed while still maintaining a view of all surroundings. It is identified as warrant, as it is most often used during raids and law enforcement warrant service operations.

☐ *Hostage Rescue*—This style is effectively a full out run, and requires a higher degree of concentration and the ability to immediately adapt and overcome obstacles.

What not to do—As stated earlier, tactical movement is a relatively complex issue, which requires proper training and practice in order to become proficient. Therefore you are encouraged to seek out professional instruction to learn the proper techniques. That said, there are a few simple considerations which should be remembered at all times when moving within this type of environment.

☐ *Never cross over your feet and legs.* If the need to move laterally (sideways) is present, it is better to place the first foot off the ground in front of and in alignment with the toes of the second foot and then slide the second foot in the direction you wish to move. This technique is similar to a half shuffle, and allows you to maintain visualization of the target or immediate threat area while you move.

☐ *Never stop.* Once you have decided to move, do not stop or attempt to turn back. Many a squirrel have moved on the happy hunting grounds because of this attempt. If your selected location becomes unavailable, you should have another in mind for an immediate transition.

☐ *Never exaggerate your steps.* If you would like to trip, this is a good way to do it. Remember what was said at the top of this section about balance? Well it applies here. If you over exaggerate your steps, your body will be out of alignment, and you will be more susceptible to being thrown of balance.

While there are other considerations, this section is presented only as an overview, and again you the reader are encouraged to seek out professional instruction.

ADVANCED COMBAT SHOOTING TECHNIQUES

In the realm of combat shooting there are two tiers. The first tier includes basic combat principles techniques and which we discussed earlier and the second includes more advanced principles and techniques which we will discuss now.

As with all the techniques outlined in this book, none should be attempted without the direct supervision of a qualified instructor or trainer.

Now that we have covered basic combat principles and techniques it is time to move on to more advanced concepts and principles which include the following.

- ☐ The immediate threat concept
- ☐ Dealing with multiple targets
- ☐ One handed shooting & reloads
- ☐ Anti-carjacking techniques

Immediate threat concept

The immediate threat concept includes an assessment of the area in which the threat is located as well as the specifics of the aggressor who presents the greatest level of threat. Say, for example, during a room clearing operation, three armed individuals are encountered. The first is approximately 40 feet away and is carrying a shotgun; the second individual is 30 feet away with a tire iron; and the third is 25 feet away with a knife. In this scenario, the one who poses the greatest or most immediate threat, would be the individual with the knife. Why? This individual would pose the greatest threat because, while close to equal distance to the second individual, he is armed with a knife, which immediately increases the risk factor of death or serious injury. For this reason, this is the individual who should be engaged first, if retreat is not an option.

Dealing with multiple threats

In the scenario above, three attackers were presented. Assuming the most immediate threat has been identified and engaged, what about the other two? How should they be dealt with if we operate under the assumption that deadly force is authorized/necessary to stop all three of them?

While there may be differing opinions about this, I will relate the method I prefer.

☐ Engage the immediate threat, first, with a single round to the COM.

☐ Engage the second most immediate threat with a single round to the COM.

☐ Engage the third most immediate threat with a single round to the COM.

This entire procedure should occur within a matter of seconds, and after the first series of engagements is completed, the shooter should return to the first threat to continue the engagement if necessary. While I *personally* prefer to use a controlled pair with each engagement before returning my attention to the first threat, this action will often require more time than is available. Therefore, unless you are confident that you can use the controlled pair technique very quickly, I would recommend performing the steps as outlined above.

Body armor/drug response

There are times when a single round, or even a controlled pair or hammer, fired into the COM of an assailant fails to stop an aggressor. In this section, we will cover a combat shooting technique that is useful if the first two rounds are unsuccessful in removing the threat. We call this the body armor/drug response because it is most often necessary when the aggressor is wearing body armor or is under the influence of narcotics, both of which might make it more difficult for rounds fired to the COM to prevent further aggression.

While this is not a situation that will likely occur for the average person practicing self-defense, it is something I teach to all my students.

There are two ways to perform the body armor/drug response technique. They are outlined below.

Body armor/drug response technique 1: This involves placing an initial controlled pair into the COM of the aggressor, followed by a follow-up round fired to the head or CNS.

The following illustration demonstrates the body armor/drug response technique 1.

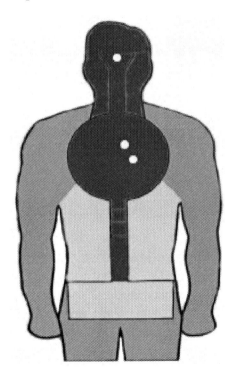

Body armor/drug response technique 2: The second technique also involves the placement of a controlled pair into the COM, but is followed by multiple shots to the pelvic area.

The following illustration demonstrates the body armor/drug response technique 2.

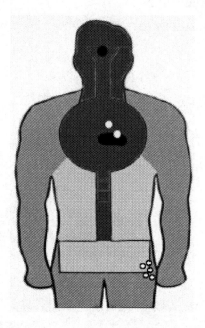

Warning: this technique is *not* recommended as a primary engagement technique. This is because the pain this type of injury may cause the aggressor, while extreme, may not be enough to fully incapacitate the aggressor especially if they under the influence of narcotic substances. Even if the pelvis is shattered and the aggressor is on the ground, they may still be capable of continuing to engage you with a weapon. In addition, the pelvic girdle is one of the strongest bones in the body. As such, you will need to deliver a series of well-placed shots to cause the damage necessary to incapacitate your attacker, and the level of accuracy needed to do this may not be achievable based on your level of skill, unless properly trained.

Here is a scenario that better explains when the body armor/drug response techniques, described above, would be useful.

You are out for an evening with a friend, wife, etc. While

walking down the sidewalk, you observe a suspicious looking individual who appears to be under the influence of drugs or alcohol. At this point, you do not think he has spotted you, as he is still approximately 75 to 100 feet away. However, because you are situationally aware and prefer to avoid a confrontation, you cross the street and alter your path to your destination. Too late! The individual sees you and begins to yell unintelligibly at you. You quicken your pace in an effort to retreat, and while doing so, your companion twists her ankle and can no longer walk. You immediately move into a defensive posture, which includes preparing for the possible need to use force to defend yourself and your companion. You continue watching this individual, who is now advancing at you more quickly, and you observe that he has something in his hand that catches and reflects light. You yell for him to stop but he continues to advance toward you. You decide that he poses an immediate threat and believe that lethal force is justified.

You draw your weapon and fire a controlled pair into the chest of your attacker. To your surprise, he continues to advance. He is now within 15 feet of you and you observe that he has a knife. What do you do? Do you continue to fire at his chest? While this may work, it is important to remember that by this point, he is way too close. What's more, the two rounds you fired into his chest already did not have the desired effect, nor even slow him down. This may be due to body armor protecting his chest, but you just don't know. What you do know, is that the closer he gets to you, the greater the danger to yourself and your companion. At this point, it would be my personal choice to discharge a round into the head or CNS of this attacker and end the conflict.

Now that we have discussed the why and when to use these techniques, we will move on to how to use them.

Performing the body armor/drug response technique 1:

☐ Draw your weapon and fire a controlled pair into the

COM of the aggressor.

☐ Then return to the high ready position and scan the area for additional threats.

☐ Breathe as normally as possible while you monitor the aggressor's actions. If the initial two rounds fail to at minimum incapacitate the aggressor, re-align your sights on the aggressor and fire one additional round into the head or CNS.

Performing the body armor/drug response technique 2:

☐ Draw your weapon and fire a controlled pair into the COM of the aggressor.

☐ Then return to the high ready position and scan the area for additional threats.

☐ Breathe as normally as possible while you monitor the aggressor's actions. If the initial two rounds fail to incapacitate the aggressor, re-align your sights on the aggressor and fire several additional rounds into the crest of the ilium, or hip. (Remember, the crest of the ilium is located on the outside edge of the hip, and if broken, will cause instant pain and will cause your aggressor to drop to ground. Again, this is *not* recommended as a primary engagement technique for reasons we have already mentioned).

One-handed shooting

There are several reasons for shooting with one hand: injury, position of cover or concealment, or the necessity for speed which may not permit the use of a two-handed grip. (Originally, the pistol was designed as a one-handed weapon, and was meant to be used by soldiers on horseback who would need to hold the reins of the horse with one hand while engaging the enemy with the other).

While this is an important skill to have, far too few

instructors teach it to their students. For this reason, I have chosen to include it in this section.

The technique used to perform a one-handed draw is virtually identical to that used in a two-handed draw. However, with two-handed shooting, both the support and master hand hold the weapon while the trigger is pressed. While in one-handed shooting, the support hand does not grip the weapon, rather it is brought to the center of the chest where it remains unless the need for other actions become necessary.

All other body position requirements of the one-handed shoot are identical to that of the two-handed shooting: grip, foot positioning, locking of the wrist, elbow/shoulder placement, etc. all remain the same. In addition, with both one and two-handed shooting, you must remember to keep your head level, bringing the gun up to your eyes, with knees bent as you lean into the recoil.

The illustration, below, demonstrates the proper position for the one-handed shooing technique.

One-handed reload

Occasionally, an individual will need to reload his weapon

with one hand. This may be due to injury, body position or some other consideration. The following will present you with an overview of how this can be done.

For simplicity's sake, we will discuss this technique using a scenario in which you have sustained an injury to your support side arm. You are under attack and behind cover. Your weapon round count is low and you decide that you have an opportunity to perform a reload. How do you do it?

One-handed reload technique 1:

☐ Kneel down with your support leg bent at a 45 degree angle and your master knee on the ground.

☐ Place your weapon in the crook behind the knee of your master leg.

☐ With your leg holding the weapon in place, release and remove the old magazine with your master hand.

☐ Store the old magazine in a pocket or simply leave it on the ground while you retrieve a fresh magazine with your master hand.

☐ Insert and seat the fresh magazine.

☐ Grab the weapon with your master hand and resume your firing position.

The following illustration demonstrates this technique.

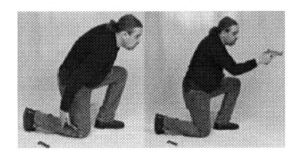

Performing the one-handed reload technique 2:

The second technique for performing a one-handed reload is used when the weapon is empty. This requires a variation on the first technique because you now have an additional requirement of releasing the weapon slide to chamber the cartridge, once the fresh magazine has been inserted.

First we will cover the recommended way to do this. Then I will share with you an alternate method, but one which I do not recommend for reasons which will become clear later.

☐ Kneel down with your support leg bent at a 45-degree angle and your master knee on the ground.

☐ Place your weapon in the crook behind the knee of your master leg.

☐ With your leg holding the weapon in place, release and remove the old magazine with your master hand.

☐ Store the old magazine in a pocket or simply leave it on the ground while you retrieve a fresh magazine with your master hand.

☐ Insert and seat the fresh magazine.

☐ Re-grip the weapon, firmly, with the master hand and place the weapon's front sight against the heel of the master side boot or shoe. Push the weapons front sight against the heel of your boot or shoe, which will cause the slide stop to disengage and chamber a cartridge.

☐ Resume your firing position.

An alternate method for disengaging the slide stop would be to simply use the slide stop itself to release it. However, when you do this you must change your grip on your weapon and this is difficult with one hand. The extra time it takes to do this without dropping the weapon is time you don't have during a conflict. Remember: during a violent confrontation, time is as great an enemy as is your attacker or opponent.

There is a third method that some use as well, but I do not recommend it. This involves pressing the front site against a belt buckle to cause the slide to release. The reason this is not recommended is because it requires placing the muzzle of the weapon in dangerous proximity to your own body. Additionally, it can be difficult to correctly line up the front site against such a small area.

The following illustration demonstrates the preferred method for performing a one-handed reload on an empty weapon.

The CJDT (carjacking defense technique)

I designed this technique specifically for use during a carjacking scenario; however, it can be used any time you are in a seated position.

The CJDT involves the series of steps outlined below. Again, this technique should never be attempted unless you have first been trained, and have practiced it, under the supervision of a qualified instructor.

- [ ] While seated, your first move is to push back your attacker. If you are in a car, you should use the vehicle door to push your attacker away from you. If you are not in a vehicle, use your support hand to push your attacker away.

- [ ] As you push forward, lean your body forward as well in order to access your weapon.

- [ ] Retrieve your weapon with your master hand and move it to the midline of your body while your support hand joins it to perform a two-handed grip.

- [ ] Present your weapon to your attacker using a modified Weaver stance. Align your sights and, if necessary, discharge with a hammer to the COM of your attacker.

The Need for Advanced Level Training

I have been a weapons and tactics instructor for civilian, security, and law enforcement personnel for the past eighteen years. I have also owned a public shooting range, and I have had the opportunity to speak with a vast number of people who carry, own, or use firearms for a variety of reasons. Sadly, however, the majority of these people, even those who come to the range regularly, have never been properly trained in the defensive use of a handgun. Yet these same people were required to take a firearms safety course, prior to obtaining their pistol permit carry, and I fear that these people maintain a false sense of security.

In this section, I will present some of the reasons why I believe that anyone who carries or owns a firearm for self-defense should give strong consideration to attending an advanced firearm-training course from a competent instructor. I will also provide some guidelines to use when selecting an instructor. But before we discuss choosing an instructor, I will explain, more fully, the reasons that I believe advanced training is so important.

If you were to ask most people who own firearms for defense whether they know how to use their handgun they would likely say "Yes, I took a class before I applied for my pistol permit." Unfortunately, while these courses *are* an important part of firearms ownership, often they do not teach students the much needed skills, such as the proper method of drawing a weapon from its holster, how to clear a stoppage or jam, or even the difference between cover and conceal-ment, much less how to use each correctly.

Another topic which is not covered in these safety courses is how to properly carry your gun and how to defend against having your gun taken away and used against you. Other topics of advanced instruction which are not covered, but are among the primary reasons people obtain pistol permits in the first place, include: how to correctly investigate the proverbial "*bump*" in the middle of the night in your home, how to avoid tragedy to you or a loved one who comes home just a little later than expected, how to use a flashlight in conjunction with a handgun, and how develop a plan in the event of a home invasion.

Another issue that is overlooked in these preliminary training sessions is how to choose the right weapon for home defense. While these are considered by many to be *advanced* techniques; they are, in my professional opinion, minimum requirements for anyone who carries, or owns a firearm for defense.

The ability to function under extreme stress

These days it is easy for someone to say: "If I was ever attacked I would draw my gun and shoot." The truth is that we can never know if we are capable of using deadly force until the moment we feel that our lives are in danger.

Taking the life of another human being is a major decision and one that cannot be taken lightly. In addition, people tend to lose their ability to function effectively when under extreme stress. Think back to a time in your life when you were so terrified that you couldn't move. How long did it take you to compose yourself before you were able to either address that which frightened you or run away? That unit of time is equivalent to the time you will have to make a decision regarding life and death. If it takes more than two seconds, your attacker will probably win the confrontation. (Remember, it is not enough to survive the confrontation, you must "*win*" at all costs.) It is for this reason, more than any other, that proper training is so important. The desire to fire a weapon at another human being is something which *cannot* be taught. Yet it is a personal, moral, and ethical question that each individual must answer when placed in a violent situation.

Advanced firearms training, if taught correctly, can assist you in dealing with increasingly stressful situations so that when, and if, the time comes, you will be prepared to act swiftly and effectively, by reverting back to training received.

Such training, if done properly, starts off slowly, with a minimal amount of stress, in a relatively relaxed environment. However, as the class proceeds, the student is exposed to increasing levels of stress. At the same time, the timeframe permitted to complete the drills is reduced. By subjecting the student to this gradually increased level of stress in a controlled environment, the student will gain a better understanding of how to manage their stress and function efficiently in a hostile situation.

Justifiable use of force laws

As an instructor, the most common questions I am asked regard the use of force. Although each state has different laws with regard to the use of physical force upon another, all state laws have common features. The basic safety class, mandated for permit applicants by several states, does not include instruction on these issues. In addition, new permit applicants only receive a copy of the state statutes with their application and are expected to understand what they read. Unfortunately, the laws are not clearly defined in most cases, and many people will not understand what they are reading unless a trained professional explains it to them. (Remember, the law was written by *lawyers*.)

This is where a competent instructor comes in. An instructor who has years of experience, in both carrying and instructing in the use of firearms, can relay not only his personal experiences and opinions, but can present the laws in simple English. In addition to clarifying the laws, an instructor can act as an expert witness or recommend other professionals (such as attorneys) if the need arises. Simply put, given the current hysteria surrounding firearms, anyone who owns or carries should strive to have as much training, and as many professional relationships as possible, with others who are properly trained in the use of firearms.

Hands on training vs. books or videos

It is almost impossible to pick up a magazine and not find an ad for instructional video tapes or books covering everything from CQB (Close Quarter Battle) tactics for S.W.A.T. teams (Special Weapons and Tactics) to how to shoot quickly and accurately. While these forms of instruction have a place, they are not the best way for a novice to learn the correct way to use a firearm in a defensive situation. And while a tremendous amount of information can be obtained from books and videos, even if the exercises contain therein are practiced regularly, there is no competent professional instructor around to evaluate and correct any errors which may be performed. This can create an extremely dangerous situation by instilling a false sense of security. Therefore, my position is that books, videos and the like should be used only as reference materials.

Another problem, which often occurs when the reader attempts to practice skills obtained via a book or video, is that most shooting ranges will not permit this type of practice and will restrict the student to static firing only.

In short, the importance of a qualified instructor cannot be overstated, for if mistakes made in training are carried over into an actual confrontation, the results *can* be devastating.

Selecting an instructor

Unfortunately, since the events of 9/11, instructors and training schools have quite literally popped up all over the country. Some of these schools are excellent, while others are less than optimum, and in some cases downright dangerous.

In this section, I will attempt to provide you with some guidelines to use when selecting an instructor, as well as point you to some of the warning signs to be aware of. It is important to remember that even if someone was a Navy S.E.A.L., Army Ranger, Delta Force Operator or cop on a

S.W.A.T team for half of their life, *this does not make them an instructor.* Additionally, even if someone has been shooting for 40 years, this does not make him an instructor.

To support this I offer the following story which appeared in the newspaper "The Tennessean." This story was written by a reporter who attended a firearms training program. The reporter described a technique, which was demonstrated to the class, causing a firestorm.

The individual in question claimed to be a former FBI agent, and stated that he used this technique to assist students in learning to overcome the fear and anxiety that typically accompanies the decision to press the trigger of a firearm while aiming another human. The instructor took an unloaded handgun, handed it to the student and told the student to point it at his (the instructor's) head *and squeeze the trigger.* Now, I can tell you that any instructor with any degree of functioning gray matter knows that this is a recipe for disaster. *Remember: one of the first rules of handgun safety is that you always consider a weapon to be loaded and you never point the muzzle at anything you don't want to shoot.*

Another example involves two students from a very well known and reputable training school who returned to their hotel after class and decided to practice what they had learned earlier in the day. They had been practicing drawing from the holster, and apparently had neglected to verify, at least three times, that their weapons were unloaded. The end result was the death of a student. Was this the fault of the instructors or school? In my opinion, No. Not entirely, anyway. The problem is that the students failed to adhere to basic fundamental training principles--principles which I am sure were covered in excess.

Now we'll move on to some of the criteria you should consider when selecting an instructor.

☐ *Is the instructor a professional trainer or just someone who is out to make a buck, as a part time endeavor, or as a second form of income?* This is a fairly common situation, especially for gun dealers. While they may be technically certified, it is important to remember that their primary business is the sale of firearms.

☐ *Does the instructor make available to prospective students copies of his certifications or other training documentation?* As I stated previously, since the events of 9/11, significant numbers of instructors and trainers have popped up virtually overnight. While many may be qualified, many more will not be. From my personal point of view, any instructor who is resistant to provide a prospective student or client with copies of his credentials for review should be considered suspect. This is not to say that they are a necessarily a bad instructor, but I would consider hesitation to do so as an indication that they have something to hide. At *Williams Associates Protective Services LLC* we have a standing policy which permits the student or perspective student to review all instructor credentials upon request.

☐ *Can/will the instructor provide references from other students who will provide an honest opinion of their services?* With this recommendation, it is important to remember that an instructor can handpick people to provide references. While this, in itself, should not be a major concern, it is something to consider. I always encourage new or prospective students to visit other students with whom I am working, and allow them time to talk amongst themselves. This is in addition to providing contact information for previous students and clients who are willing to provide feedback.

☐ *How long has the instructor been an instructor?* As stated earlier, while field experience is important, it is *not* the only criteria for a good instructor. Again, even if someone has been shooting for 40 years, that does not necessarily mean he/she is a good instructor. Conversely, I have known people who have never served in the military, law enforcement or other similar occupation, and have only been teaching for a few years, yet they are exceptional instructors. The key is found in the individual personality of the instructor.

☐ *What is the average ratio of student to instructor?* Generally, it is best to have no more than five students to each instructor. However, the fewer students per instructor, the better. In any type of educational situation, I believe that one-on-one or two-on one training provides the very best learning experience. A potentially poor learning experience would be found with an instructor who is just out to make a buck. Granted, we are all in business to make money, but I have always taken the position that the student's needs come first. For me, training is not just an occupation, but also a way of life. I often tell my students that if I were to win the lottery tomorrow, I would still be at the range (once I returned from my vacation) to continue their training. This is not the case with the instructor who is teaching simply to bring in a little extra money. I have personally observed instructors who will run training classes with 25 students and only one assistant. In my opinion, this is a recipe for disaster and indicates a blatant lack of consideration for the students.

☐ *Does the instructor continually seek to receive or update their training in the newest techniques?* Ok. Like virtually everything else, changes occur every day with a new stance, grip, or other technique, which are introduced to the training or shooting community. Some of these techniques are valid and should be given consideration, while many others are not and should not be. However, it is the responsibility of the professional instructor to stay up-to-date on these changes and to teach those which are sound so that the student will be provided with the latest techniques of personal protection available.

☐ *Does the instructor carry personal liability insurance?*

Have any student injuries occurred during the training provided by the instructor? Even if there have been accidents during training, this should not automatically cause you to think that particular instructor is poor. However, it *should* cause you to take the time to investigate further, in order to determine the cause of the accident(s). While I really hate to keep pounding the part-time instructor, again I return to him for an example. I once performed a very unscientific poll of instructors who train people as a hobby or second form of income. I asked them if they carried personal/professional liability insurance, just in case a student was ever hurt. The overwhelming majority of them said they did not. But what was perhaps even more frightening, was that many of them asked me "What is that?" While the occurrence of accidents and/or serious injuries during civilian training courses are relatively rare, they do happen.

To me, a sign of professionalism, as well as general business sense, is to always maintain insurance which will protect both the instructor and the student, in the event of a serious injury.

☐ *Is the instructor trained in emergency medicine or first aid or does he rely upon the response of Emergency Medical Services (EMS) in the event of an emergency?* Here is the reality. As I said above, serious accidents and injuries within firearms training programs are actually quite rare; however, they *do* occur, and when they do, time is of the essence. An individual who is wounded by a bullet will often go into a state of shock very rapidly, *and this condition is life threatening.* Depending on the location of the training, the response times for EMS can exceed 10 minutes. While this may not seem like a long period of time, I assure you that when you've been shot, it's a very long time indeed. This is not to say that every instructor must be an Emergency Medical Technician or paramedic, but at minimum he should be trained in basic first aid.

☐ *Will the instructor be available after the class to answer questions if they arise, or will there be an additional charge for these services?* While this does not appear to be a frequently occurring problem, there are instructors who feel that once the class or program is completed, their obligation to the student ends. In my professional opinion, this could not be further from the truth. If one where to ask any of my previous students if they felt they could contact me after they completed a course or training program with me, I am very confident that they would recall what I told them at the conclusion of the class: "If you have any questions, or require any assistance, I do not care if it is a year from now, I am simply a phone call or e-mail away." I consider this to be another sign of professionalism, as well as good business sense. Once you have provided knowledge, skills, or information to another, in many ways you are part of their life. And as such, you hold a level of responsibility to them. Many of my students continue to tell stories to new and potential students of how I accompanied them, at no charge, to a local gun store to make their first purchase. Now, I am not implying that if another instructor is not willing to do this that makes him wrong, only that I *am* willing to do this because I truly feel the student comes first.

☐ *Does the instructor "bad mouth" other instructors without justification?* In the firearms training community, like virtually any other business, the competition is fierce. As a result, some instructors will use any tactic available in an effort to make money. Ask yourself a question. If you walked into a gun shop or other location and inquired about a specific instructor or school, and were told a litany of bad things, only to then be told "Well, we offer the same training and do it better," wouldn't you be a *little* suspicious? A true professional doesn't need to make somebody else look bad to get your business. So, would you really want to trust someone like this to train you in a skill, or set of skills, that you're going to use to defend your life?

☐ *Is the instructor arrogant toward their students or does he try to be supportive?* This is an area which really bothers me. I have always taken the position that arrogance and knowledge do not necessarily go together. I will admit that I have witnessed a great deal of arrogance from instructors myself; however, this has been in the context of a closed community, which has never been seen by students. There is no place for arrogance on the part of an instructor in a training environment. The role of the instructor or trainer is to impart knowledge and help with the building of skills. It is not a forum in which to brag about their personal adventures or talk down to those who have come to partake of their knowledge. While so-called war stories and tales of exploits *can* be a benefit to the instructor for the purposes of maintaining interest in the material, such things should never be presented in an effort to make the student feel poorly about his own skills. The philosophy, which has served me best, is that when I am working with a student I am not just training them, I am training *with* them. So, while I do know more than they do in this particular area, I do not know everything, and there is a strong chance I will learn something from them as well. Additionally, I have always told my students that I will never lie to them. If they should present a question to me that I cannot answer on the spot, I *will* look into it and get back to them with the answer.

This, in my opinion, is another sign of professionalism.

☐ *Are handout materials provided to supplement the training program?* The axiom "A picture says a thousand words" definitely applies here. The average person comes to a training program for one reason: to learn. In many cases, programs are held on a weekend or in the evening. After a hard day at work, the last thing anyone wants to do is be writing hundreds of pages of notes on lecture material being presented. Therefore, I always provide a handout packet to my students. It not only helps them follow the material as it's being covered, but it provides them with reference material for future use. In my experience, most professional instructors will do something similar to this, as it is an important training/teaching method.

☐ *Does the instructor or school insist that their way is the only way to do things?* Or do they seek to provide a foundation and encourage their students to modify the techniques to better fit their individual body configurations? Many years ago, when I was just starting out as an instructor, I had the opportunity to train with an extremely knowledgeable and skilled trainer. This man had been involved with the British S.A.S. for many years and was involved in a series of high speed/high risk rescue operations in the 1980's. He imparted a bit of advice to me which, to this day, I still adhere to. He said "The wise instructor will present the student with a foundation from which to build, but will never attempt to build the house." What this means to me, is that it is my responsibility as an instructor to present the skills to the student, and then encourage them to modify the techniques to fit themselves. Unfortunately, there are a lot of instructors who insist that the way they do things is the *only* way and any deviation from it is wrong. In my opinion, they are the ones who are wrong. I personally would much rather see my students improvise and *win* the conflict, than spend so much time concentrating on doing it my way that they waste precious time and get killed in the process.

While the preceding list is by no means intended to be all-inclusive, it is provided in an effort to assist the reader in what to look for when selecting an instructor from whom to receive training in firearms and tactics. The bottom line is this: there are many talented and skilled instructors, trainers and schools to choose from; however, as with any goods or services, prior investigation is worth the time and effort it takes whenever you are preparing to make an important decision.

The student's responsibilities

Just as the instructor or trainer has a responsibility to present accurate information to the student, the student also bares a degree of responsibility within the training environment. The following is a listing of the *most* important responsibilities of the student.

☐ The student must *want* to be part of the class.

☐ The student must want to *learn* the material and must be willing to *practice* the techniques presented.

☐ The student must *follow instructions* and if unsure, must always be willing to *ask* for clarification.

ESOTERIC PRINCIPLES AND CONSIDERATIONS

In this section we will discuss topic areas which you may perceive as unusual or strange. However, I have placed them here in an effort to help you better understand some of the principles which warriors throughout history have used to help them maintain their spirit and ultimately win their wars and conflicts. Make no mistake about it, beyond the current wars our country is involved in on foreign soil, each day every citizen of this country and the world is a potential casualty in an ever present war between those who abide the law and those who do not. It is for this reason that this section has been added, in hopes of imparting to you some of the principles needed to win any violent confrontation you may encounter.

You have taken your required training, obtained your license, purchased your first gun, holster, and ammunition. You have gone to the shooting range and fired thousands of rounds of ammunition. You have even taken some advanced level training courses to insure that you know what you are doing and are proficient in your skills.

You carry your gun everyday and everywhere you go. You boast to close friends that you can shoot super fast and accurately and that no one better mess with you or your family because you can stop them on a dime. And so you go through your new life as an armed protector of those you love and the principles of freedom you hold dear. But do you really know your weapon? Do you know the minor almost unnoticeable flaws within its action? Do you know which ammunition will work the best and which will cause failures? Can you immediately notice when something is wrong, when a part is about to fail or is becoming tired from extended use? The answer to these questions, is probably not. It is this inner knowledge which separates the true operator/warrior from the average person or *wannabe*. Now, I am aware that the statements above will offend and anger some readers, but unfortunately there is no other way to present the truth. So this information is presented in the hopes of helping those who do not understand the mindset of the warrior so that they may learn to become as warriors themselves.

In the previous paragraph, I stated that true warriors will know even the slightest defect or change which takes place with their weapons. Now I will present you with some information on how to gain this insight for yourself. The following guidelines are not intended to be a begin all and end all, rather they are intended to help the reader on the path of enlightenment.

To start with, a true warrior will be proficient with and will likely own and use multiple weapons platforms. In addition, a true warrior will always maintain a favorite above all others and will try to have this weapon available at all times. It is this weapon which we shall identify as our primary weapon. Now, before I go any further, the term primary will usually refer to the main weapon carried such as a rifle with a soldier, and in some cases a secondary weapon such as a pistol will also be carried. However, for the purpose of this section we will refer to the primary as your favorite sidearm. Now, how does one come to know their weapon to this degree as listed above?

The first step on the path of this enlightenment is to provide your primary weapon with a name. Yes, I said to *name* your weapon. Be it a favorite knife, gun, sword, baton, etc., provide this primary weapon with a name. Now, you must be asking yourself as you read this, "Is this guy nuts?" In answer to your question, no I am not. If you were to talk to any combat soldier they would tell you of others (even if they did not admit it themselves), who have named their weapons.

In addition, in some military circles, the custom of naming one's weapon is encouraged, for the reasons stated above. In fact, this practice dates back to the Roman Empire, where centurions often named their swords or the feudal Japanese samurai believed their swords were the soul of their warriorship. You are probably asking yourself, what does giving my weapon a name have to do with knowing it? The answer to this question is a little complicated, but I will try to make it as easy as possible.

To better understand the important people in our lives, we try above all else to know these people: their likes, dislikes, when they are happy, when they are sad, when they are tired, when they are in pain. It is this principle upon which the naming of one's primary weapon is built. Now, I am not implying that a weapon or any other piece of equipment possesses any emotions, after all it is just an inanimate object. However, the emotions of the operator can play a large part in becoming *as one* with the weapon.

The name you choose should be a name which holds a special, personal, and private meaning to you alone. It is not important that others understand the relevance. After the proper name has been determined, you must seek to learn everything you can about your weapon--not the manufacturing process or the reviews issued by experts or other users of the same weapon--but the intricacies and inner personality of *your* primary weapon.

Okay, I realize I said "inner personality" of the weapon and just a minute ago I said that a weapon cannot have any emotions. Well, they don't, however all mechanical devices will have certain quirks which can be *called* a personality. You need to learn these things the same way that you would seek to learn the personality of a friend or lover, by interaction.

Carrying each day will cause you to eventually not notice the added weight, but it will be noticeable when you are not carrying. Think of it this way: if you spend virtually all of your free time with your lover, then when your lover is not with you, you feel a void.

Likewise, in any relationship, you will seek to determine your lover's likes and dislikes. This, in turn, will lead to a more harmonious relationship. The same applies to your weapon. Slow repetitive static shooting, where you feel the pressure build against the trigger just before firing; the movement of the slide, and to which side the recoil will cause the weapon to twist; these are the little intrinsic personality traits one must seek to learn, in order to become *one with* the weapon and truly know it. Shooting multiple different types of ammunition and loads will also tell you which type of ammunition/loads the weapon is most comfortable with.

In the end, the only way to truly know your primary weapon of defense is to personalize the piece of machinery by bestowing upon it a name which is special and personal to you alone, and considering it an intimate part of your own existence. By doing such you will begin to treat the weapon as you do your loved ones, paying close attention to every detail. And in return, your weapon will always be loyal to you and be ever ready to serve you with a minimal fear of failure.

OTHER CONSIDERATIONS

Throughout this book we have discussed the various principles of combat, necessary mindset and techniques which are needed to properly and effectively defend oneself from attack. We have not, however, discussed what happens after the conflict, alternative methods of defense or the consideration of using or carrying a back-up weapon. So it is here where we will discuss these points.

After the fact

A topic of equal, if not greater importance, than how to handle a conflict, is the protection of the victim from the legal implications and ramifications inherent in the use of lethal force. As discussed in other sections, during a violent confrontation where lethal force is deemed necessary, there will be very little time to make a decision which will ultimately determine the fate of another human being. Let's assume that a confrontation has escalated to a level requiring the use of lethal force, the decision has been made to deliver this level of force, and the action of lethal force is carried out. What next? Although every state will have differing laws and regulations, it is safe to assume that all states and jurisdictions will require anyone who is involved in a lethal force engagement to notify the proper authorities. It is this area which we will be focusing on throughout the following section.

As human beings we are emotional creatures. As a result, we tend to react without forethought when a traumatic event, such as the use of lethal force, is necessary. This is often linked to the enormous amount of mental stress which is place upon an individual with the realization that they have just taken a human life. After such an event, the first words stated by you, to the authorities, can and often will be considered as *a formal statement* regardless of the mental state you are in at the time. There have been numerous cases of individuals who used justifiable lethal force in self-defense situations, yet who were subjected to aggressive prosecution attempts based upon the initial statements made by them, to the police, immediately following an event.

While the intent of this section is not to advise anyone to be uncooperative, or to give the appearance of guilt or innocence when speaking with authorities in the aftermath of a lethal force encounter, it *is* my intention to provide you with some basic guidelines for dealing with the authorities in the aftermath of such event.

Miranda rights

We have all read about, or seen in the movies or on television, a person being questioned by law enforcement officials. So we all know that the first step required under the Constitution of the United States is for them to be read their *Miranda rights.* The following is the actual text of the Miranda warning, which must be read to, and acknowledged as understood by, *anyone* prior to official questioning by law enforcement authorities.

1. *You have the right to remain silent and refuse to answer any questions.*

2. *Anything you say may be used against you in a court of law.*

3. *As we discuss this matter, you have a right to stop answering my questions at any time you desire.*

4. *You have a right to consult with a lawyer before speaking to me, and to remain silent until you can talk to him/her, and to have him/her present when you are being questioned.*

5. *If you want a lawyer but cannot afford one, one will be provided to you without cost.*

6. *Do you understand each of these rights I have explained to you?*

7. *Now that I have advised you of your rights, are you willing to answer my questions without an attorney present?*

The preceding are the Miranda rights which must be read to all persons questioned by law enforcement officials, whether they are considered a suspect or witness *prior* to questioning by the authorities.

Again, it is not the intention of this section to advocate any behavior outside what is permitted under the terms of the Miranda warning. The first line of the Miranda warning states that you have the right to remain silent and refuse to answer any questions. You should exercise this right to a degree.

In the aftermath of a violent confrontation, which involves the use of any degree of force, the following actions should be taken immediately to prevent further complications, including you being injured by mistake. To begin with, when the authorities arrive, you must follow all of their commands without hesitation. You will likely be ordered to drop your weapon. Comply with this order. You may, if the responding officer feels that his safety is in question, be ordered to kneel on the ground with your hands on the top of your head, and may be temporarily restrained via the use of handcuffs or some other form of physical restraining device. Do *not* offer any resistance and comply immediately with all instructions given by the officer. If you feel that the officer's requests were unwarranted, comply with them anyway. The matter can be addressed at a later time, with your attorney.

The next line of the Miranda warning states that anything you say may be used against you in a court of law. (This is why so many people involved in these types of situations are so aggressively prosecuted.)

When asked by an investigator to elaborate on the events which have taken place, your response should be as follows:

"My name is____, my date of birth is____, my address is____, and my social security number is____. At this time I wish to exercise my Miranda right to remain silent and confer with an attorney prior to offering any statement or answering any further questions."

At this point you must be thinking to yourself, "But what about when the officer tells me that things will go easier if I just tell him what happened?" The simple answer to this question is to respond with the information as stated above and never provide any additional information beyond your name, date of birth, residence address and social security number, *prior to speaking with an attorney.* You must ignore, while remaining respectful and non-confrontational, the request to answer any additional questions regardless of the topic area.

In some cases, investigators will attempt to develop information based upon a seemingly routine or unrelated conversation with you which has no relevance to the event. Remember: Anything you say to the authorities can, and often will, be used in court as evidence against you. Now, this is not to say that the authorities are intent upon finding you guilty of a crime; however, the officer must report all information he receives in the course of an investigation and this information will be reviewed by the prosecutor who will determine if the use of lethal force was within the requirements of the law. So any information which can be misconstrued, quite often, will be.

While every violent confrontation will be different, by exercising the rights and behaviors outlined in this section, a tremendous amount of additional hassles and problems can be avoided. This is simply because if no information is presented, there is nothing to be misinterpreted or misconstrued.

Now, I do not pretend that this course of action is easy to adhere to. Nor is it the intention of this section to imply that by following these guidelines you will not face any legal hassles or complications, rather those complications will be *reduced* by the simple act of keeping your mouth shut. As stated above, you have a right to remain silent and confer with an attorney prior to answering any questions. Exercise these rights!

Secondary/back-up weapons

An issue of contention among many within the handgun-carrying community is the use of a *secondary* or *back-up* gun also referred to as a *BUG*. In this section, we will discuss the rationale, as well as the pros and cons of this practice. Please understand that nothing contained herein is intended to advocate any particular practice by any individual. The information is merely presented as the opinion of the author, for the purposes of providing the reader with the information needed to develop his/her own informed opinion.

Rationale for carrying a back-up weapon:

Carrying a single firearm, on a daily basis, for the purpose of self-defense, can pose a series of difficulties. These difficulties include the restriction of one's wardrobe, the additional weight which must be carried around, the bulkiness, and the ever present concern of the weapon being exposed to view by the public; which could lead to the authorities being contacted, creating additional problems. Now, for those who consider the carrying of a *back-up* or *secondary* weapon, these problems are increased two-fold. However, the individual must personally weigh the hassles and concerns verses the need for personal defense. Here's an analogy to help better explain the rationale behind the decision to carry a *back-up* weapon. Think of a hospital. There are a series of machines used to monitor patients and assist the surgeon in the procedures being performed. Some of these machines are classified as critical, which means that failure of the machine during the middle of a surgical procedure could have significantly dangerous repercussions. For this reason, those machines have back-up systems that can be deployed, as needed.

Another example of redundancy, which can be found in a hospital as well as large corporations, and even some homes, is a back-up generator. The function of the back-up generator is to provide electricity in the event of a power outage. By this point you are probably asking what is the relevance of back-up generators and hospital equipment in relation to the carrying of a *back-up* or *secondary* firearm for the purposes of defense. To answer this question we need to first understand exactly what a firearm is. Simply put, a firearm is a mechanical device; and as such, is inherently prone to failure. Of course, there are high-grade firearms which have a lower probability of failure; however, by the very nature of the device, failure of some form, at some point, is inevitable.

An example of this can be found in the automotive world. A brand new vehicle is not very likely to have problems which will cause the vehicle to break down. Yet examples of this occur on a daily basis. Why? Because a vehicle is a mechanical device with articulating components and parts interconnected to perform a specific action or function. As such, all are prone to effects of wear and the environment. An example of this is the radiator. The radiator of a vehicle is filled with fluid which is used to cool the engine; however this liquid is subjected to high temperatures, therefore, evaporation *will* occur. If left unchecked, the fluid will evaporate, thus allowing the engine to overheat and seize.

The consideration applies to firearms. Each time they are fired, they are subjected to both high temperatures and high levels of pressure. And although most shooters will maintain their weapons and watch for wear or damage, it is still possible for parts to break without notice. While this is normal, the issue of timing is of great concern. If this failure occurs during a target shooting session, no problem.

However if this failure were to occur during a confrontation, the results could be disastrous.

The solution to this problem is found in *redundancy*. Just as an operating room is equipped with a second identical machine so that in the event of failure by the primary machine the secondary is readily available, a shooter in a violent confrontation can benefit from the same redundancy.

Another example of this principle can be found in the equipment used by S.C.U.B.A divers, where redundancy is key to a safe and enjoyable dive. This fact was demonstrated to me when I was engaged in a dive with a group of friends.

We had planned to dive on a WWII German U-Boat, the U-853, which was sunk off the coast of Block Island. Because of the depth to which we would be diving and the amount of bottom time we wanted to spend, we decided to perform what is known as a *multi-stage decompression dive*. This involves multiple stops, at multiple depths, to decompress prior to surfacing. To safely perform this type of dive, we were required to build in back-up systems to our back-up systems, which included separate *pony bottle* air tanks and regulators, in addition to the primary and secondary regulators attached to our main air tanks. Ideally, the air contained within the main tank would have been sufficient to support the entire dive without the need to resort to the back-up pony bottle. However, on this particular trip the back-up system of the pony bottle saved the life of my partner.

Here is what happened. We all arrived at the hotel the night before the dive. That night, we made our final major equipment checks, which we would repeat yet again in the morning. (Okay, I realize I just said it was our *final* equipment check; however, I did not name the technique). In any event, the next morning we headed to the docks to meet the charter. The member of the group who was to be my partner appeared to be fine. He was excited to be on the trip, but showed no signs of anxiety or any other condition that gave me cause for concern.

In addition, we had partnered before and I was comfortable with his skill level. Upon arrival at the site, the seas were a bit rough; however, not enough for us to abort the dive. We entered the water and proceeded on the trip down approximately 130 feet to the bottom. The dive itself went very smoothly and no problems were discovered until our ascent to the surface. During the second of four decompression stops, my dive partner signaled to me that he was almost completely out of air. I examined his gauges and his main bottle was totally empty. What's more, his pony bottle contained only 100 PSI (pounds per square inch) of air. Considering that we needed to remain underwater for another 15 – 20 minutes before we would be able to surface safely, we were presented with a real emergency. Upon examining my gauges, I was surprised to see that while I had spent the same time below surface as my partner, I still was maintaining approximately 2000 PSI in my main air tank.

I was not in any immediate danger of running out of air myself, and the idea of performing an emergency ascent was not very appealing. Therefore, I decided to provide my pony bottle, which was full, to my partner to use for the remainder of the way to the surface.

Once back on the boat, my dive partner informed me that for some reason, which he did not understand himself, he had begun to breath much faster and deeper than normal while under water, thus expending greater volumes of air. We all agreed that it was "just one of those things" and proceeded back to the docks.

However, if it had not been for a redundant back-up air system, the situation could have been much worse.

The same principles apply to firearms, regardless of their configuration: pistol, rifle or shotgun. Although meticulous maintenance and cleaning will assist in the prevention of failures, there can be no guarantee of flawless performance. And unfortunately, the time a firearm is most likely to fail is when it is needed the most.

So what can be done about this situation? The only solution is redundancy. This means carrying a *secondary* or *back-up* weapon. Now it should be understood that this back-up weapon need not be a full-sized large caliber firearm, as the intended purpose of this weapon is for use as a last resort when no other alternative remains.

Recommendations for a suitable back-up firearm:

In this section I will give examples of some of my recommendations for a suitable back-up firearm caliber. Again, as stated above, it needs to be understood that a back-up firearm does not need to be a full size weapon or large caliber.

The first calibers we will discuss are the .22 caliber and 25acp. Both of these calibers are available in extremely small frame firearms, which will fit in the palm of the hand. However, of these two calibers, the .22 caliber is in my opinion, a more reliable and effective choice. While the reasons for this are fairly extensive, the main reason is the velocity of the projectile. When a .22 caliber enters soft tissue, the high velocity of the projectile will quite often deflect off of bones within the body and bounce around within the internal cavities; thus causing a higher degree of soft tissue injury. While the larger 25acp will also cause soft tissue damage (due to its increased size and weight), the projectile will move more slowly and its ability to deflect will be decreased, causing less tissue damage.

With the smaller calibers, the deflection of the projectile within the body is essential for the purpose of causing sufficient soft tissue damage and will increase your ability to incapacitate your attacker. However, neither of these calibers should ever be used as a *primary* defense weapon, due to their inability to cause significant trauma to the body of the attacker.

The next caliber we will discuss is the 32acp, which is a fairly common back-up weapon. Some of the primary reasons for this are the size and weight of the firearm, which fires cartridges that are quite often similar, if not identical to, the size of the frames found in weapons chambered for the .22 caliber or 25acp. However, the amount of energy contained behind this larger sized cartridge, coupled with the caliber of the projectile, makes the 32acp a better choice as a back-up or secondary defensive weapon. (While there may be a bit of contention and debate over the effectiveness of the 32acp, I can say with complete assuredness that under the right circumstances, like any other caliber, a .32acp can and will be very effective).

This will be better understood in the context of an event which took place several years ago, when I witnessed the effects of the 32acp as fired through a *Seecamp* semi-automatic pistol. The following is a summary of the events which took place.

On a warm summer evening, a friend and I decided that we were going to go out to visit a few bars. Prior to heading to our first bar, we made a stop at a mutual friend's shop, where we met with an individual who was known by my friend, but not to me. This new individual asked if he could join us for the evening. Now, generally I would have avoided letting an individual I did not know come out with me, as I am the type that likes to know those around me whenever possible. However, since this person was known by my friend, I felt that it would not be a problem. By the end of the night, however, I was to learn that this was a really big mistake.

We began by patronizing a few of the local establishments. Then this new member of our party suggested we visit a bar which in the next town over. Neither myself nor my friend offered up any major objections other than to insist that this new member of our group drive, as our plans had involved us staying in town and visiting bars we could walk to. So, we headed off to this new bar. Not long after we arrived, I began to feel sick and so I headed out for some fresh air. I sat in the car, hanging my head out of the door, feeling ill, just as a police patrol car was driving around the parking lot. After I recovered from being sick, I sat back in my seat in the vehicle and began to doze. The next thing I remember is the sound of running and a voice saying something like "Let's get the hell out of here." Then the vehicle started to move. I awoke, briefly, and asked, "Are we home yet?" to which I recall being told "No, not yet. Soon." I dozed off again, only to be awakened by one hell of a surprise. My mouth was full of blood, and my left leg was pinned up underneath the dashboard. To make matters worse, I was so disoriented that when my friend sprang up next to me and startled me, I almost hit him.

We both managed to exit the vehicle and when we did, we found ourselves in what I can only describe as a *scene from a bad movie*. There was a woman screaming "He shot her, he shot her!" And another unknown individual was lying on the ground writhing. I finally spotted the individual we had come with. He was also lying on the ground, with his arm draped across his face. While we still did not immediately understand what had occurred, both my friend and I ran to a pay phone and contacted 911. Upon arrival of the police, we were placed in separate vehicles, and brought to the police department to provide a statement. I provided my statement, which was very close to what I have outlined above, and was told to wait.

I later found out that while I was waiting, the officer (who had observed me outside in the car earlier) had spoken up and informed the others that there was no way I could have been involved in the incident because of my condition.

Later, I was informed regarding the details of the events that occurred that night. Apparently, this third individual (who had asked to join us on our night out) had done so with a very specific intention in mind. His girlfriend had broken up with him and she was seeing someone new. This individual knew that she would be at this particular bar and wanted an excuse to go there. The situation got out of hand and a fight had broken out in the bar, which had spilled out into the parking lot. My friend and this third person ran to the vehicle where I was dozing, entered it and began to drive. However, instead of returning home, the driver of the vehicle (who was this third person) drove his vehicle into the parking lot of the bar, striking his old girlfriend's new boyfriend. I do not recall if he also shot him or not; however, I do know that the boyfriend was hit by the vehicle and suffered a severely fractured leg. This third person then exited the vehicle we were all in, and proceeded to shoot his ex-girlfriend in the face, killing her instantly. He then shot himself in the temple. This did not kill him, but it did cause him to be permanently paralyzed. The weapon caliber used in this incident was a 32acp Winchester silvertip.

The next, and final smaller caliber we will discuss, is the 380acp. The 380acp cartridge made famous in the James Bond movies of the 1970's and 80's is actually what is called a 9mm *kurtz* or *corto,* which means short. An extremely popular caliber in Europe, the 380acp cartridge is, in my opinion, the absolute *minimum* caliber which should be considered for general defensive purposes. However, as technology has evolved, the calibers which were once only available within the larger frames (such as 9mm and 45acp) are now available in a smaller frame size.

Thanks to this technology, shooters can now be afforded virtually the same level of ballistic performance that was once only available in a full- sized firearm.

As with the primary defensive firearm, the back-up or secondary firearm must also be of sufficient quality to avoid failures. At this point you may be thinking that if the back-up weapon is also a mechanical device, isn't it as prone to failure as the primary? The answer to this question is yes, and no. It *is* a mechanical device, and therefore it is prone to failure. However, if it is of sufficient quality the chances of failure are reduced based on its relatively limited use.

Statistically, the more a weapon is fired, the greater the

chances of failure. As your secondary weapon will be used mostly for practice, it should fail less often than your primary weapon. Also, remember that your secondary weapon is not intended to be brought to the range for the purpose of target shooting. It is meant to be a last resort defensive device when a primary weapon is either unavailable or has failed. (Although the back-up weapon *should* be test fired periodically, to ensure proper feeding and function, which will also reduce the chances of failure).

In this section, we have focused mainly on secondary and back-up firearms of the lower calibers and smaller sized frames. However, there is no law which states that a back-up weapon must be limited in size and/or caliber. The size/caliber of your secondary weapon is really dependent upon the circumstances under which it is to be used. An additional determining factor will be your ability to properly carry the weapon (either in an exposed or concealed manner) and the added weight involved in carrying the additional weapon on a regular basis.

How and where to carry a back-up pistol:

Another area of controversy involves the method in which a back-up or secondary pistol should be carried. In this section we will discuss the various options available and the considerations needed in making a proper decision with regard to how to carry the secondary weapon.

As with the primary weapon, the first and most important consideration is the shooter's ability to access the weapon in a time of need. That said, I will extend this piece of advice: While ankle holsters may seem like a good idea, a tremendous amount of training is required to effectively and properly use this type of system. The major drawbacks with the use of an ankle holster include the additional time needed to access the weapon, the physical movement required to access the weapon and the restriction of certain types of clothing when utilizing this type of system. If your wardrobe requires you to wear loose fitting pants (such as those found with a business suit or uniform) the problem of clothing restriction will be reduced. However, if your general wardrobe includes the use of denim jeans or similar material and the cut of the pants is a straight line configuration, access to the weapon will be dramatically impeded while the attempt is made to pull up the pant leg (which may require both hands) thus increasing the time it will take you to grip and draw the weapon.

Balance is also a major consideration when using an ankle holster. Unless you are seated or supine when you attempt to draw the weapon, it will be necessary to bend forward at the waist to retrieve the weapon, which will place you off balance. For these reasons, the use of an ankle holster to carry a primary weapon is *strongly* discouraged and only considered for use with a back-up weapon, in the absence of any other reasonable alternative, and even then extensive training and practice should be engaged in.

Some individuals choose to carry a back-up or secondary firearm in their pocket or in the small of the back. Both of these methods also contain hazards which we will now discuss. In the case of a pocket, unless the back-up or secondary weapon is a revolver, the chances of a stoppage or failure after the first round is fired from within the pocket are significant. You may wonder why anybody would try to discharge a weapon while it is still in a pocket.

The reason is that a back-up weapon is only going to be used when the situation has degraded to a full-scale combat scenario and your primary weapon has failed. In such a situation, the commodity of time is not at your disposal. Therefore, you may be forced to discharge your back-up weapon from the compartment where you keep it, and this will often cause problems with semi-automatics, as the restriction of space can prevent them from cycling correctly and can cause a stoppage.

The small of the back is another popular area where

individuals often chose to carry their primary or secondary firearm. The main problem with this method of carry is the inability of the individual to adequately protect the weapon. This is because the shooter's arms and hands may not provide the necessary leverage and mobility to stop someone who is attempting to grab the weapon.

Therefore, as with all other techniques, extensive training is required to utilize this method of carry appropriately. By this point you are likely saying, so where do I carry this secondary weapon? I'm afraid I don't have a tried and true answer to offer you; however, I will extend the following advice: A back-up or secondary weapon should be readily available on your person, so as not to become a burden yet still be available if needed. What does this mean? Basically, it means that there are several different devices/methods for the carrying firearms on one's body.

Choosing the right method is an individual choice, but that choice *should* be guided by the wisdom of a professional trainer or instructor who possesses the proper training in specialized deployment techniques.

As we can see, there are several variables which need to be taken into consideration with regard to back-up and secondary firearms. And while carrying an additional firearm is important for redundancy in the event of a failure of your primary weapon, the decision to carry a back-up must be carefully considered.

In addition, while carrying a secondary or back-up weapon is something I do recommend, that statement is tempered with the understanding that extensive training and periodic practice on the part of the student are *essential* to the proper deployment of these weapons within a combat situation.

Deploying a weapon from the concealed position

The principles of drawing from the concealed position are virtually identical to the 5-point draw, with the exception of a few additional steps. These steps are necessary to make sure the concealing garment is moved out of the way before the weapon is discharged.

☐ *Point 1*—The master hand is moved toward the concealed weapon with the heel of the palm pressed firmly against the body, allowing for the covering garment to be moved out of the way while the body is turned or bladed in the direction of the master side.

☐ *Point 2*—The master hand secures a firm grip on the weapon, and releases the safety or security strap, if present, while the support hand moves to the center of the torso and waits.

☐ *Point 3*—The weapon is drawn from the holster while canting the muzzle forward causing the front sight and muzzle to snap forward when cleared from the holster.

☐ *Point 4*—Once clear of the holster, the butt of the weapon is moved across the front of the body, held as closely as possible to the body, until it meets the support hand in the center of the torso, where a two handed grip is performed.

☐ *Point 5*—Both arms are extended forward in the direction of the target.

☐ *Point 6*—The sights are aligned and, if necessary, the weapon is discharged.

The following illustration demonstrates the steps required to deploy a weapon from the concealed position.

Proper concealed carry

When carrying a weapon in a concealed fashion, there are several considerations which must be adhered too. The following listing outlines two of the most important of these considerations:

1. *Rapid access to the weapon*—If you cannot access the weapon when it is needed, then it is of no value to you for the purpose of self-protection. An example of an incorrect location for a handgun is a woman's purse, as it will require more time to access it and additionally it will be harder to protect.

2. *The correct holster for the weapon*—If the weapon is held in a holster which is not fitted to hold it, or if the weight of the weapon causes you to constantly alter its position or adjust it, this will draw unwanted attention to you. Additionally, if it is not a comfortable fit, you will not carry the weapon and again, it will be of no use to you.

The position of the holster

The ideal location for carrying a handgun is on the hip. The main reason for this is that this position allows you to most easily protect the weapon from being grabbed by an aggressor. There are three styles of waist line carry. They include the *pelvic carry*, where the holster is positioned in the front of the hip close to the torso, the *kidney carry,* where the holster is positioned behind the hip over the kidney, and finally the dreaded S.O.B. or *small of the back* carry position. This is the most common and the most dangerous carrying technique. It is also the technique that is most often used incorrectly. While this carry position can be one of the most comfortable positions, the down side is that when a weapon is carried in this position, it is very difficult for the wearer to adequately protect the weapon. This is due to the lack of leverage provided by the arms and the subsequent inability of the wearer to reach around the back and engage an aggressor with enough strength to defend the weapon.

ALTERNATIVE METHODS OF PERSONAL DEFENSE

There are alternative techniques for personal protection that do not include the use of firearms. In this section, we will discuss one of the more common tools: defensive chemical sprays. Why would someone choose a spray over a firearm? There could be several reasons. Among them are a person's age, physical ability, religious or spiritual beliefs and profuse government restrictions which might prohibit an individual from owning or carrying a firearm for personal protection. Additionally, there are times when it is simply not feasible to carry a firearm. But personal security need not be compromised because of this.

In this chapter we will discuss the chemical agents that are generally available to civilians and law enforcement personnel for use in self-defense.

Defensive chemical sprays

The three types of defensive chemical agents which are most common will be covered in this section. The first, which is also known as *tear gas,* generally goes by the trade name *mace*. What is *not* generally known, is that under the trade name of mace, there are actually two very different chemical compounds. Both can be effective if used during a violent confrontation; however, they must be used carefully as both are capable of causing permanent injury. As such, they usually require evaluation and government clearance prior to being released for sale for use by private citizens. In fact, in many jurisdictions, civilians and non-government agencies are prohibited from using these chemical agents.

The third, and perhaps most popular defensive chemical agent, is actually not a chemical at all. Unlike CN or CS (described below) which are manufactured compounds, OC which stands for *oleoresin capsicum* also known as *pepper spray*, is actually considered more effective and safer than the preceding two compounds. The following will provide a quick overview of each of these compounds.

Chloroacetophenone (CN):

CN was developed in Germany in 1869 and is a *lachrymator* agent, meaning that the primary effect produced by the agent will be on the lachrymal structures of the eyes. It is these structures which are responsible for the production and release of tears. When CN crystals are pulverized into a powder, they can be used against an attacker in a conflict situation. However, it is important to keep in mind that using CN against an attacker, while better than nothing, may not provide the desired level of incapacitation. The effects of CN include:

- ☐ Profuse tearing;

- ☐ Voluntary closure of the eyes;

- ☐ Mild nose and skin irritation;

- ☐ A mild psychological effect of panic.

Orthochlorbenzalmalononitrile (CS):

CS was created in the late 1920s by British chemists. However, it was not until thirty years later, when CS was used to quell civil disturbances in Cyprus, that it was recognized for its potential as a less than lethal weapon. Today, we commonly refer to CS as mace. However, CS differs from CN in several ways, as can be seen from the following list. The effects of CS are listed below.

- ☐ Discomfort and burning to any exposed skin or tissue.

- ☐ Physiological and psychological effects (which may vary greatly from one person to another).

- ☐ *Some* will experience severe burning of the eyes and exposed skin.

- ☐ *Some* will experience involuntary closure of the eyes, which may be overcome with intense determination.

- ☐ Sinuses and nasal cavities will generally drain profusely.

- ☐ *Some* will experience tightening in the chest and feel as though they are having a heart attack.

- ☐ In higher doses, dizziness, nausea and vomiting are common. (CS can actually stimulate the pain receptors 10 times more than CN).

- ☐ Often severe panic will occur.

- ☐ Persons subjected to CS will often also experience mental confusion and/or disorientation.

Oleoresin capsicum (pepper spray):

The first tactical use of pepper has been traced back to approximately 2000 BC in China. Red pepper would be dried and finely ground, then wrapped in rice paper. The rice paper would then be set on fire and hurled in the direction of the opposing army. Pepper-dust particles would rise with the heat and blow into the enemy's faces causing choking, burning and temporary blindness.

During the 1930s, the U.S. military developed the original *oleoresin capsicum OC* from the oils and waxes of cayenne pepper, but could not find a practical method of delivery. During the late 1960s, an aerosol-based OC spray helped defend postal carriers against aggressive dogs. It wasn't until 1991 when the DEF-TEC Corporation developed a totally organic, non-flammable propellant carrier. It's marketed as *First Defense*. Because OC is derived from a natural source, it requires only limited government oversight. In fact, the Food and Drug Administration considers it a consumable compound.

The heat effect of *oleoresin capsicum* is measured in *scoville heat units* and a chart comparing the intensity, of various types of pepper is found below.

Pepper	Scoville Heat Units
Habanero	200,000-300,000
Tabasco	30,00-50,000
Cayenne	35,000
Jalapeno	3,500-4,500
Bell & Pimento	0

The following table explains the practical meaning of the scoville heat unit rating:

0-5,000: Mild	5,000-20,000: Medium
20,000-70,000: Hot	70,000-300,000:Extremely Hot

It is important to note, that in addition to the standard heat or scoville heat units of a given source, it is possible to *increase* the natural intensity of this compound by adding sugar to the solution. Additionally, be cautious of clever marketing practices which label products as containing 10% pepper spray or 5% pepper spray. While it may appear as if the higher percentages advertised would mean that a particular product is more potent than another, this is actually not the case.

The true level of compound intensity is based on the active ingredient, identified as *capsaicin.* Capsaicin is the ingredient responsible for the actual heat found in peppers and associated plants. To make this point, check out the comparison, below.

☐ *Brand X Pepper Spray—* 10% OC concentration with 0.18% capsaicin

☐ *Brand Y Pepper Spray—*5% OC concentration with 0.92% capsaicin.

Which brand would be hotter? The answer is Brand Y, as the amount of capsaicin it contains is higher.

Anatomical considerations:

In order to better understand how *oleoresin capsicum* works to incapacitate an aggressive individual, it is important to understand the anatomy of the human eye and its surrounding structures. This is because the effects of defensive chemical sprays are generally focused on the eye area. The following definitions are provided to assist in this goal:

Eyelids—The eyelids are simply flaps of skin which are attached by facial muscles and are designed to both protect the eye as well as to help clean the surface and maintain moistness while blinking.

Sclera—The sclera of the eye is generally referred to as the "white of the eye."

Cornea—The cornea of the eye is really another protective feature of the eye which is used to protect the lens of the eye.

Lachrymal Gland—The lachrymal gland of the eye is an organ which is used by the body to create tears.

Lachrymal Duct—The lachrymal duct is a structure commonly referred to as a *tear duct* and is a physical structure located in the far corner of the eye close to the nose. As the name implies, this is where tears are released onto the surface of the eyeball.

Tears—While tears are not truly a structure of the eye, because of their importance we will include them here. Tears serve a series of very important functions.

Tears clean the eye and maintain moisture on the surface of the eyeball, which lubricates the surface.

Mucous Membranes—These membranes are a lining within body passages such as the nose, sinuses and certain structures located in the back of the throat and are used by the respiratory system to assist in preventing foreign material from entering the body.

Sinuses—The sinus cavities are also used in conjunction with the respiratory system, and are actually open spaces which contain tiny hair like structures called *cilia*. They are designed to help move the mucosa, which is intended to help clean the air as it passes into the body.

The Conjunctiva—The conjunctiva of the eye is the thin transparent tissue that covers the outer surface of the eyeball. Beginning at the outer edge of the cornea, the conjunctiva covers the visible part of the sclera and lines the inside of the eyelids. It is nourished by tiny blood vessels that are nearly invisible to the naked eye.

The following illustration depicts the structures of the human eye.

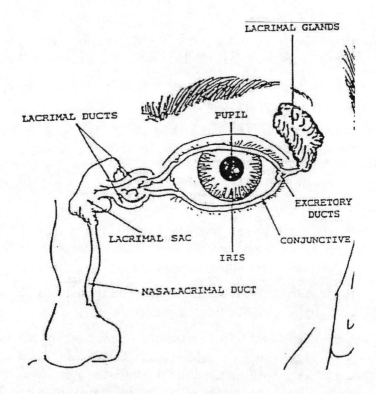

How OC Works:

When applied to the face or exposed skin of an attacker, *oleoresin capsicum* causes an intense burning sensation. When it comes in contact with mucous membranes or tissues, OC causes an involuntary muscle response: the eyes are automatically forced closed and the lachrymal glands become irritated and tear excessively. The effects of this stimulation also will irritate the inner wall of the nose and sinus cavity, forcing mucous to drain out immediately. While not normally life threatening, the effects of OC usually destroy an attacker's will to fight, as they will either attempt to escape, or fall to the ground fairly quickly. In addition to the physical effects, OC usually will leave an attacker feeling intense panic.

Now comes the warning. While OC is considered effective, it's not a sure-fire defense. Authorities consider it between 80% - 85 % effective. Most of the problems with OC occur with regard to its application.

Some years ago, while I was employed at a nightclub, an individual managed to smuggle a can of OC into the club. The OC was contained in a fogger unit, which is designed to disperse a large cloud of the agent, over a wide area. This individual dispensed a large cloud of pepper spray within the club, which was full of people. While one would expect a mass panic, this was hardly the case. Although about 20 people did leave the club choking, signaling to my partner and me that something was wrong, there was no mass exodus for the door. Unfortunately, my partner and I were required to try to make our way into the club to investigate. We managed to enter about 10 feet into the club before we were forced to return outside. What we observed, however, was quite surprising. Despite the presence of OC, the majority of the patrons continued to sit and eat, apparently unaffected by it. We managed to open the back door and air out the club and within a few hours everything returned to normal.

But the point is, if most of the patrons in this club did not even stop eating when exposed to OC, it can't be considered a sure-fire defense weapon.

Interestingly, OC was *originally* marketed as a bear repellant. And currently many use it to deter aggressive dogs. Unfortunately, the pain OC causes can actually make an aggressive animal even *more* aggressive. So if you decide to use pepper spray against a dog, just be prepared for the possibility that the dog might still attack, and take appropriate measures to retreat as quickly as possible.

Dispersion devices:

Commercially available defensive aerosol sprays are generally available in three forms, which are discussed below.

Stream—Just as the name implies, a streaming composition will release a stream of the agent. This will typically have an effective range of 5' – 12'. While susceptible to the effects of wind, a streaming composition is easier to use than a fogger, for example, if you are attempting to direct a controlled release in the direction of an attacker.

Fogger—A fogger will release a cone of the agent in the direction of the attacker. This cone also will maintain an effective range of 5' – 12' but is extremely susceptible to the effects of wind, and great caution must be used with this dispersion method to avoid self-contamination.

Foam— A relative newcomer to defensive spray dispersion systems is the foaming system. This method of agent dispersion combines the effects of a stream with the added benefits of a heavier carrier, which consists of a foaming material which is more resistant to wind than either a streaming agent or a fogger. It also causes the agent to stay in place more easily. The added benefit of a foam dispersion system is that because the foam stays on the attacker, cross contamination is possible when the attacker attempts to use his hands to wipe away the agent. This type of dispersion system also often includes the addition of a UV dye, which assists law enforcement officials in identifying an attacker who has been sprayed and has managed to leave the scene.

Generally, law enforcement tends to use the fogger dispersion system for crowd control. Hikers may also find this particular system useful for protection against wild animals, such as bears. For personal protection, most people favor the stream or foam dispersion systems.

When instructed in the use of the stream or foam dispersion systems, you will likely be told to use a series of 2-5 second bursts. I will present you with a bit of reality: when you are in danger, you will not follow these instructions. Therefore, I will offer you some alternative methods for using the OC systems, which I believe are more easily used under stressful circumstances.

The high-low method

The defender activates the canister and applies a constant stream of the agent while moving up and down from the attacker's waist to face and back again. Because it's hard to miss the body, and more of the agent will come into greater contact with the attacker, this method offers perhaps the best deployment against an attacker. It is also easier to apply, as it relies heavily on the natural movement of the body when faced with a violent confrontation, which is to raise ones hands. Provided that you are situationally aware, it would not be unreasonable for you to have your canister in your hand prior to being confronted. Once the confrontation occurs and the decision is made to defend yourself, you simply depress the actuator switch while raising your hands in the direction of your attacker.

The side-to-side method

The defender again releases a constant stream of the agent, but instead of moving from the attacker's waist to their face, the defender sweeps from shoulder to shoulder. While this method tends to waste more of the agent, it does apply a liberal dose of agent to the attacker's face. Unfortunately, this technique requires that you are fully prepared to engage a potential attacker as your body movement is not as natural as it is with the high/low method.

OC and the laws of self-defense:

States have varying laws with regard to the use of defensive sprays. For this reason, you should check the statutes in your area before purchasing or carrying any of these compounds. However I can provide you with a general overview of when a situation has escalated to allow for defense with OC. Among protection specialists we call this *placing a weapon within the force continuum.* The force continuum is a chart used to determine when, and to what degree, force is justified.

The following is a graphic illustration of the force continuum.

As with any escalation of force during a confrontation, control begins with a command or physical presence. Often, just the arrival of another individual can diffuse a situation. If not, the next level of defense is verbal direction. You, or someone else on the scene, orders the attacker to stop. It usually takes an authority figure (police, MP, boss or a very physically overpowering individual) for this to work. Up to this point the force has not been physical; it is at this point when it is generally recommended and accepted that OC (and only OC) be used as a defensive chemical agent.

Because CN and CS are chemical compounds which have the potential for permanent injury, they must be placed higher on the continuum. Most experts agree that the use of CN or CS should fall in or directly under the level at which a lethal weapon would be used. In other words, if you fear for your life or safety and would feel justified defending yourself with an impact weapon or firearm (if you had one), then you will likely be warranted in using CN or CS against an attacker.

In the end, the decision as to which type of self-protection method you use is your own. I hope this information about an alternative option is helpful.

Health, first aid and decontamination:

Any time OC is used, as with any weapon, certain medical considerations must be addressed. While I'm not aware of any evidence that would contraindicate the use of OC against people with heart conditions, asthma or the like, there is a *potentially* life threatening medical emergency which can develop. This is called *postural/positional asphyxia*, and is directly related to the positioning of an individual who has been exposed to defensive chemical agents. If, because of their physical position, they are deprived of oxygen, the result can be death. So while I won't go into great medical detail, I'll just say that the condition can be life threatening and must be watched for.

For this reason, the police or Emergency Medical personnel must be notified immediately after OC is used, so that they can monitor your attacker for the onset of this condition.

Now, before I get into the application of first aid and

decontamination techniques, you should understand that when acting as a civilian in self-defense, it is not your responsibility to render first aid or to begin the process of decontaminating your attacker. However, you *are* responsible for the effects of the agent deployed. And in any case, if you, a family member, or an innocent bystander are ever caught by an accidental discharge of OC, you should know how to initiate decontamination protocols. Therefore, I have listed them below.

- ☐ Call 911 and request an ambulance.
- ☐ Ensure that the affected individual is seated upright.
- ☐ Remove any contaminated clothing.
- ☐ Apply copious amounts of water to the affected areas.
- ☐ Monitor the individual for breathing difficulty.
- ☐ Immediately upon arrival of EMS, advise them of the compound used and the steps you have taken to begin the decontamination procedure.

Knives

In this section, we will discuss the use of knives both as an adjunct to, and as a substitute for, carrying a traditional firearm.

While we will not discuss the specific strikes, blocks or other techniques, we will discuss the reasons why carrying a knife is important for anyone who is concerned about personal safety.

Pros:
Sometimes you just can't carry a gun.

Even though you may have obtained your permit to carry a firearm, there will inevitably be times when it is simply not practical for you to do so. For example, say you are traveling across state lines on business or vacation. Although several states have a permit or license system in place, if you do not have a permit from that state or a state with reciprocity, you cannot legally carry a firearm there, unless it is secured in such a way as to comply with federal law regarding the transfer of firearms across state lines, which reads as follows:

TITLE 18 Sec. 926A. Interstate Transportation of Firearms

Notwithstanding any other provision of any law or any rule or regulation of a State or any political subdivision thereof, any person who is not otherwise prohibited by this chapter from transporting, shipping, or receiving a firearm shall be entitled to transport a firearm for any lawful purpose from any place where he may lawfully possess and carry such firearm to any other place where he may lawfully possess and carry such firearm if, during such transportation the firearm is unloaded, and neither the firearm nor any ammunition being transported is readily accessible or is directly accessible from the passenger compartment of such transporting vehicle: Provided, that in the case of a vehicle without a compartment separate from the driver's compartment, the firearm or ammunition shall be contained in a locked container other than the glove compartment or console.

And if you *are* in compliance with these federal laws, your gun will be useless to you because it will be required to be secured away from your control (i.e. in the trunk), in a secured container, unloaded, with the ammunition stored *separately*. By the time you managed to un-secure, load and prepare for its use, you will be dead!

So, an alternative is to carry a knife. In most jurisdictions, folding knives (although regulated for the length of cutting surface, which should not exceed 3" – 4") are considered completely legal for carry without a permit or license.

People generally fear a knife more than a gun.

Although a knife is not typically thought of as a primary

defensive weapon, the truth is that most people will fear a knife more than a gun, and the simple display of a knife by someone who knows how to use one, can often be a deterrent to an attack. This might surprise you, but think back to your own past. Have your ever cut yourself on a piece of glass or a kitchen knife? If you answered yes, then you already know what it feels like. It hurts, and it can hurt like hell, depending on where and how deeply you are cut. I assure you that the bad guy will be thinking of this as well, when he realizes that he is up against a knife-wielding opponent, who appears to know what they are doing.

However, the display of a knife must be considered in the same manner in which one would consider displaying a gun for defense. In other words, if you draw your knife during a defensive situation, you must be aware of the following:

☐ You must be in fear for your life.

☐ You must know how to properly use the knife within a combat situation.

☐ You must be prepared to use deadly force.

☐ You must be close enough to your attacker to effectively use the knife on him (which means you've already made two mistakes: first, you let him put you in a confrontational position and second, you let him get way too close).

☐ You must be prepared for the fact that, if engaged, there will likely be a great deal of blood to deal with.

If any of the above criteria are not met, do not attempt to use your knife for defense. If you do, you will likely be arrested for assault, or the person you are trying to stave off will take the knife *from* you and use it *on* you.

Ease of concealment.

Unlike a pistol, a knife is very easy to conceal and can still be readily available for immediate use. With a pistol, a holster is needed, the weapon will usually dictate your wardrobe, and the possibility of accidental display is higher. Also, when people see a folding knife in someone's pocket, they generally will not be as alarmed as they would if they were to see a firearm. Most folding knives are designed for defensive or tactical carry and will have a pocket clip attached. This allows the knife to be carried in a pocket, in a very *low profile* manner, while still allowing for immediate access in an emergency.

Multiple uses, easy to justify, less maintenance required.

Carrying a knife can be useful for a variety of additional tasks and chores aside from defensive purposes. This is why it is fairly easy to justify, to a police officer or other official, why you carry the knife in the first place. Granted, all of us have both the right and the obligation to protect ourselves from harm; still, there are those in positions of power who seem to believe otherwise.

If the police were to question you and discover that you were carrying a small folding knife, they would likely subject you to a 5-minute interview. Whereas, try informing a cop that you are carrying a pistol, and you will likely get a 10–20 minute interview and be subjected to an array of additional questions--and this is regardless of whether or not you hold a permit or license to carry.

Now, the preceding is not intended to imply that one should carry a knife instead of a gun. It is simply meant to demonstrate that generally knives do not generate the same level of concern a handgun will. In fact, even if you happen to carry a knife *and* a pistol, should you find yourself in the above situation, it is a fairly safe bet that questions about the knife will be few, as the focus will be on the pistol and whether or not you are authorized to carry it.

Another benefit to using a knife for self-protection is that unlike a firearm, a knife requires very limited maintenance. Basically, all you need to do to maintain a knife is keep it clean and sharpen the edge occasionally. Whereas, a firearm should be cleaned after each use, and contains a number of moving parts which are susceptible to damage and wear.

So, now that we've covered some good reasons for carrying a knife for self-defense, we will move on to some of the inherent problems with use of a knife in a defensive situation.

Cons:
Problem # 1: The first rule of knife fighting.

The first rule of knife fighting is that no matter how highly trained you are in the use of a knife, if you engage an opponent with a knife *you are going to get cut!* This is not a pleasant thought, but it is a reality which must be acknowledged. The degree of damage you will sustain is directly related to several factors including but not limited to:

- ☐ The skill of your opponent;
- ☐ Your skill level;
- ☐ Your luck;
- ☐ Your ability to remain focused during a violent confrontation (especially when you are injured).

All of the above principles are interconnected and need to be considered when engaging any opponent within a knife fight. But again, it *must* be acknowledged that if you fight with a knife y*ou will get cut!*

Problem # 2: Blood born pathogens (Diseases)

Another serious problem with knife fighting is the exposure to blood, and lots of it. Certain areas of the human body have large numbers of near surface blood vessels, known as *capillaries.* While severing these tiny blood vessels will not cause death (or any significant damage to your opponent) they will give the appearance of the release of large volumes of blood. However, there is an upside to this. Most people rethink what they're doing when they realize they're bleeding. If you cut your opponent, even if the cut is not incapacitating, it may be enough to cause them to stop thier aggressive behavior long enough for you to safely retreat. Of course, this can also work against you if you are the one who begins to leak.

Another problem, worth consideration, is the fact that your attacker's blood, if it should enter an open wound on your body, would make you susceptible to any disease your attacker may have. Then again, which would you prefer, taking the chance of getting a disease from a stranger or failing to engage and letting that same stranger kill you then and there? It really comes down to this: Combat in any form is an ugly and dangerous business. In combat situations, people *will* get hurt. So, in the end, based upon the principles outlined above, what alternative do you really have?

Problem # 3: The requirement for extensive training.

Anyone can stab someone with a knife; however, if you are trained in both the defensive and offensive techniques of knife combat, it will make a significant difference in how the situation unfolds. Just as you require training to become proficient in the tactical use of a firearm, proper techniques in the use of a knife in close combat cannot be overlooked. When an attacker sees a knife in the hands of someone who is properly trained, he will immediately notice certain subtle signs which *may* be enough to signal him to keep his distance. For instance, someone who is properly trained will immediately position themselves in a fighting stance in order to be ready to counter an attack. Additionally, someone who knows the proper techniques for knife fighting will exude a level of confidence which will also often be evident to their attacker. Sometimes that's all it takes to cause an attacker to rethink his actions before committing to a fight with a victim who is not as helpless as they had originally thought.

SUMMARY

In this book, we have covered a wide range of topics relating to self-defense. I have attempted to use common sense and logic to address many of the principles contained herein without the over use of *buzz words* which are far too common in other books of this type, and often make them difficult to understand.

The goal of this book is to help the average person better understand, and prepare for, the violent confrontations they may face in daily life. For as much as we'd like to think we are immune from the escalating violence and criminal activity occurring every day, the truth is you just never know when you will find yourself in a violent confrontation. For this reason I have taken an extremely complex series of subjects and have attempted to present them in such a way as to make them both understandable, and applicable, to your daily life.

I hope the information in this book has shed some light on the importance of the physical techniques used in self-defense, as well as the need for an increased level of situational awareness so that you, the reader, may avoid becoming involved in a violent confrontation.

I cannot overstate however that none of the techniques described in this book should be attempted by anyone outside of the direct supervision of a qualified instructor and that failure to do so may result in serious injury or death. There is no alternative. Remember: *It is not enough to simply survive the conflict, you must win at all costs!*

The methods, techniques and tactics outlined herein are the actual techniques and principles which are taught to all students of *Williams Associates Protective Services, LLC* as well as several other professional firearms training schools; including those which cater exclusively to law enforcement and military personnel.

APPENDIX A: REFERENCE LETTERS

The letters on the following pages were sent to the author of this book by clients/students of *Williams Associates Protective Services LLC.*

Dear Brian,

When I attend the NRA Basic Pistol Permit class last October, I had only one intention, to take the class as one of the requirements to attain a pistol permit. Shortly into the day's long seminar, I began to realize that this was serious business, and learning the safety issues in carrying a firearm was only a small part of a much bigger picture. If one was going to carry a firearm for self-defense, one must know how to use it.

I was very impressed with the professional format of the class. I was also impressed that you did not give out these NRA certificates easily, and that in addition to passing the NRA multiple choice questions, you had your own ten essay questions that had to be carefully answered. And indeed, not everyone went home with their certification of completion of the course that day.

Other than firing a 22 rifle on occasion as a teenager, my experience with firearms was very limited. You strongly suggested that I sign up for training to build up my proficiency in using a pistol. It's been four months since I started training with you and last week I entered my first competition. I didn't do too badly either!

I must thank you for your patience with me, and praise you on your ability to evaluate the numerous mistakes I made during this learning process. The encouragement you give even on "bad days" is appreciated. Your own expertise in your field displays itself through precise and thorough training increasing one's competency in a timely fashion. You also make learning a lot of fun!

Thanks Brian, again, for your dedication and sensitivity that makes for a great instructor. I always look forward to our class every other week!

Sincerely,

Leslie R.

Dear Brian,

I wanted to let you know that I really enjoyed your tactical handgun I class this past weekend. I learned so much from you. The relaxed atmosphere coupled with your outstanding professionalism really made learning easy and fun. I appreciate all you've done and your availability, at any time, to answer questions and to demonstrate techniques. You and your facilities are truly outstanding, and your past experience is exceptional. I personally believe that if someone is going to exercise their 2nd amendment right, they should learn and practice all they can and you have made that easy. I would and have recommended you, your facilities and your classes to anyone and everyone that is even remotely interested in firearms and personal protection. I am looking forward to further training with you, especially the Tactical Handgun II class. Keep up the good work and thank you so much for sharing your experience, knowledge, and time.

Sincerely,

Carol W.

Dear Bryan,

In my search to begin firearms training I was unsure and intimidated to say the least. Prior to meeting with you, I had absolutely no firearms experience. After meeting with you initially, I knew it would be a great experience for me to learn from you. Besides your technical expertise, you were able to make learning something I looked forward to and still do to this day. I never felt like I couldn't ask you anything, and I attribute that to the way you handle all of your students. Your goal is to help us learn, be safe and improve our skills.

For the past 5 months, I have been under your tutelage and instruction about firearms safety, operation, maintenance, and tactical training. I have come a long way since our initial training sessions and I owe that to you. I truly value the skills you have taught me and look forward each week to building upon those. Thank you for being a great teacher.

Sincerely,

Matt M.

Dear Brian,

I wanted to write you to thank you for the wonderful experience I had during your TDH 1 class on 02/06 - 02/07/99!!! I cannot thank you enough! Your professionalism was beyond reproach! I also had a lot of fun; which in turn made it easier for me to learn.

You told us that at any time we could either call or come and talk to you, at no charge! That does not happen very often in this world today. I so value your experience, and the reputation that you carry! I would HIGHLY recommend you and your facility to anyone who is interested in expanding their own knowledge for self-protection. I would consider it an honor and pleasure to be a part of any future classes.

What I have learned from you will save my life someday, if I ever have to put that knowledge into practice. I know how MUCH I have to learn, but at least, I have a beginning. I left with a feeling of accomplishment and a little more confidence in myself. I know I have a long way to go, but with your help and guidance, I believe I can accomplish the goals that I have set for myself. Again, I wish to say thank you to you for a most empowering & enlightening experience!

Sincerely,

Susan V.

Dear Brian:

I wanted to take this opportunity for developing a customized tactical handgun defense course just for me.

I have a Connecticut concealed carry permit and own two pistols, and I feel that expert training in handgun tactical defense is absolutely essential. In fact, anyone considering buying a handgun and applying for a permit to carry, owes it to him or herself to avail themselves of your professional training.

In my search to locate an instructor to assist me in achieving my goals I found you and your school via the Internet. I am glad to have a professional of your caliber teaching me. Your level of expertise and qualifications are too numerous to mention in a quick note such as this. As the saying goes, "the more I learn the less I realize I know," so I envision continuing my training for a long time, and look forward to joining the ranks of the "advanced once a month group."

In closing, allow me to express my appreciation for your personalized attention. I would strongly recommend your courses to anyone pursuing any type of self- defense training.

Sincerely,

Shirley, C.

Dear Brian,

I just wanted to write and thank you for your instruction in the TDH-1 class I took from you. My objective in taking TDH-1 was to understand the fundamentals of the defensive use of firearms and to obtain the basic training necessary to become proficient for self defense. After completing the class I came away with:

The reinforcement of safety and the use of firearms, an understanding the fundamental use of firearms for defense, appreciation of the stress and fatigue and how it affects you in a defensive situation, and the need for continued training.

The format of the class was professionally put together. I liked the limited class size for both safety and individual attention. Obviously, safe gun handling cannot be assumed and in an entry level class like TDH-1 it is even more critical. Accordingly, I thought the limited class size demonstrated the professionalism and seriousness of firearms training.

After completing the class, you would think that you would walk away feeling that you are qualified to carry a gun for defense. My experience was quite the opposite. I came away with more respect for the training necessary to be proficient and the need for continued training. In that respect, TDH-1 is the foundation for more training and proficiency. I would highly recommend TDH-1 for anyone with a serious desire to learn more about defensive handguns.

I would qualify my statement with the words "serious desire". TDH-1 is a demanding class in terms of commitment of time, concentration, attention, and physical work. If you are serious about learning about defensive handguns, TDH-1 is an excellent place to start.

Brian, I appreciated your personal attention and look forward to training with you again.

Best regards,

Ben M.

Dear Brian,

January 1997, I took your Tactical Defense Course and I must take this opportunity to tell you, that it was a wonderful confidence builder and an eye opening experience. I have been around firearms since I was in high schools may years ago that I would prefer to forget just how long. I moved from New York City to Connecticut and obtained a Connecticut Carry Permit. Your course showed me what I didn't know about handling a handgun and then went on to teach what you should know. You have a companion manual that accompanies the course which is very comprehensive as well. The course was conducted in a manor that was fun making the intensity of the course very easy to handle.

Upon completion of the course I came away more confident and with more peace of mind carrying my firearm, with the knowledge that if I must draw a firearm, I do know how to use it. But best of all is the monthly remedial course you run it keeps the edge for me. Keep up the good work and I will be seeing you each month.

Best regards,

Jason B.

Dear Bryan,

As you know I have been training under your tutelage for the past three years. During that time my shooting skills and abilities have progressed remarkably due to your knowledge, experience, skills and patience. I now have the skill base and confidence that are essential to owning and carrying a firearm for self-defense. As with any skill, constant practice and uptake of new knowledge are tantamount. You go out of your way to accommodate my hectic daily schedule, and are is equally adept at both one-on-one and group training.

It is my opinion, that your unique style of teaching is predicated upon building the confidence of the student one layer at a time, and tailoring the training program to the individual, based upon skill level at the beginning of training. Gradually you add more complex techniques as cumulative skills and confidence of the student warrant and increase which promotes a positive learning atmosphere, giving both praise and suggestions for improvement when needed.

Before locating and seeking your help I was quite frustrated at my lack of progress, and had considered giving up shooting altogether. I now enjoy my new hobby with extreme zeal, and own an ever-growing collection of firearms. I have successfully introduced many others to the sport of shooting and my confidence and skills as a shooter continue to improve as a result of my continued training. My overall confidence as a person also continues to improve. Since I decided to train under you and believe that under someone else I may not have been able to progress so well. Most importantly I consider you to be a very good friend, and I highly recommend your services to anyone who wishes to own a firearm.

Sincerely,

Neil G.

Dear Bryan,

Once I made the commitment to get my concealed carry permit, I was left with the difficult decision of where to get the proper knowledge and training. I needed an instructor that would provide me with no-nonsense, reality-based firearm training in personal defense. Williams Associates did not disappoint!

Through Williams Associates I completed my basic permit certification course and their private year-long tactical training course. Williams Associates provided professional, comprehensive, scenario-based training. Bryans sincere concern and interest in his students' progression and achievement allowed for a very constructive and interactive relationship both inside and outside of training. I highly recommend Williams Associates to everyone from the beginner to the skilled law enforcement professional.

--John C.

Dear Bryan,

It has been about a year since I have begun training with you, and I wanted take some time and let you know how much I have enjoyed working with you. I remember our first conversation over the phone. Almost immediately I felt that you were someone I would work with. You were professional and easy to talk to. I did not know what to expect or even what I wanted to get out of firearms training. My main concern was to learn how to handle a firearm safely and to develop basic skills for defensive shooting. What I received was an instructor who listened to my needs and designed a program around what I wanted. Building skills upon skills and fostering development through deadpan analysis and supportive corrections. You never made me feel that my lack of experience was a bad thing and you met my enthusiasm head on, directing my energy down the right path. In doing so, you have helped me begin a journey towards further education and skill development that has not only been vital to me and just plain fun.

I look forward to our weekly sessions as a fun stress reliever and never as work. Without you as an instructor and friend I would never have developed the patience on my own to be an effective and responsible gun owner. Since I started training with you, I feel that my skill level and confidence has grown appropriately. The skills that I am learning are providing me with the foundation to achieve my goals. You have been available to me night and day and for this I am grateful. We have talked about may things both personal and professional. That is why I have no reservations recommending you to friends and family or anyone that wants to learn from an instructor with experience and integrity.

Your Student and Friend

Rick V.

APPENDIX B: AUTHOR'S CONTACT INFORMATION

Bryan Scott Williams, the author of this book, can be reached for additional information about training programs offered through ***Williams Associates Protective Services, LLC*** or for interview requests, by the following means:

Surface Mail:

Williams Associates Protective Services, LLC
P.O. Box 164
Derby, CT. 06418
USA
Attention: Bryan Scott Williams

Telephone: 203.924.1784
On the World Wide Web: www.wa-protective.com
E-mail: admin@wa-protective.com